Publicity to the Rescue

How to Get More Attention for Your Animal Shelter, Humane Society or Rescue Group to Raise Awareness, Increase Donations, Recruit Volunteers, and Boost Adoptions

Susan C. Daffron

Logical Express
www.LogicalExpre

D1158808

ISBN:

978-1-61038-004-1 (Paperback)

978-1-61038-005-8 (EPUB)

978-1-61038-006-5 (MobiPocket/Kindle)

Library of Congress Control Number: 2011914679

Cover photograph by Susan C. Daffron of her dog Fiona
who was adopted through Samoyed rescue.
Microphone image from iStockPhoto.com

Contents

Publicity Basics

Publicity Tactics

Section 1

Publicity

Basics

The Power of Publicity

Many rescue groups struggle to get the word out about what they do, but it's not as difficult as it may seem to get noticed. In fact, it can be easy.

Publicity is a powerful tool you can use for your rescue or humane group. In fact, publicity can be vastly more effective than paid advertising, because it works like a third-party endorsement. Whether the media is objective or not, people believe that when you appear on authoritative Web sites, blogs, newspapers, radio, or TV, it's "news." People believe the news; they don't believe advertising.

That's the power of publicity.

It's not as hard as you may think to get publicity. Here's why:

- Every day the media needs stories
- People love animals

If you can craft stories that people find interesting, you'll have no trouble getting "ink" (whether virtual or literal). Many people working for rescue and humane groups tend to think of publicity only in terms of getting people to fundraising events, but you can use publicity to go way beyond being included on basic community event calendars.

You can use publicity to:

- **Find volunteers and foster families**. If, like a lot of rescue groups, you have trouble finding new foster homes for your animals, you can use publicity to get the word out.

- **Educate the public**. As an example, outside of the animal shelter and rescue world, most people don't even know what fostering is; they've never heard the term. They don't know why spaying and neutering pets matters. Your job is to tell them!

- **Increase adoptions**. An old adage in business states that people prefer to buy from someone they know. In this case, substitute "buy" with "adopt." People need to know your group exists in order to adopt animals from you.

The bottom line is that people don't know you need foster families and volunteers unless you tell them. It doesn't have to be complicated or expensive to get the word out, either.

If you know how to get the attention of the media, the real winners are the animals. People will start to think of your group as the place to go when they need a pet.

No one wants to think about "competition," but the reality is that **most** people don't adopt their pets; they get them at pet stores or from breeders. Why? Because they know about those outlets and they are easy to remember.

Publicity can give your group the top-of-mind awareness that pet stores and breeders have now. In fact, think about the best-case scenario: people stop shopping at pet stores, and instead they come to you for their next pet. What could that mean for your rescue group and the community as a whole?

- Fewer animals die because more animals are adopted

- More space is available in shelters for homeless animals and euthanasia statistics drop.

It's amazing what can happen when you start getting the word out about who you are and what you do. A lot of people would do the right thing for their animals, if they only knew what to do.

Publicity can give potential adopters, donors, and volunteers the opportunity to know you and why the work you are doing matters. Advertising won't do that for you.

Probably the best news about publicity for cash-strapped rescue groups is that it's free! Okay, maybe sometimes it's only "almost free," but a publicity campaign doesn't have to cost a lot, and a local campaign can cost you exactly $0.

In this book you'll find case studies from humane and rescue groups just like yours. In virtually every case, they used nothing more than creativity and a little "sweat equity" to raise awareness.

Although a few of the case studies include work by professional publicists, most of the case studies are from individuals or groups who simply wanted to make a difference for the animals and took action. You'll find that the case studies highlight a lot of the do-it-yourself, grass-roots techniques I describe in this book.

I've also included copies of real press releases I have written that were picked up by the media, so you can see examples of what works. You'll see that getting media attention isn't really as hard as it may seem, even if you're not an extroverted "sales or marketing type." (Heaven knows, I'm not!)

So what are you waiting for? Let's get started!

Get Ready for the Media

Before you start trying to get publicity, you need to have three key elements in place.

1. **You need to know your story**. To be newsworthy, you have to set yourself apart from the sea of charities, services, and businesses that are competing for the attention of the media. The key to rising above the general noise level is to create a consistent, distinctive message that resonates with people. These people are your potential adopters and donors. Whatever you do needs to appeal to them.

2. **You need to have a Web site**. Ideally, your Web site should have an online media kit with information about your mission and message. Your Web site needs to be findable by people doing a Google search. Some extremely "pretty" Web sites are completely useless because no one can find them. Even a simple site can be extremely effective if it loads quickly, clearly explains who you are and what you do, is easy to navigate, and looks professional.

3. **You should have access to high-quality images**. A lot of public relations is visual. You have an amazing publicity advantage because you have adorable critters. People love animals. Find a photographer who loves taking pictures of

animals. The better the images on your Web site and printed materials, the more professional you look. Consider videos, too. Shoot videos of your adorable animals doing adorable things.

All of these pieces of the puzzle offer clues to what your organization is about. You often see the word "branding" bandied about. However, branding isn't as complex as some people would have you believe. It's really just providing an overall impression of who you are and what you represent, so people identify your group with *one* core idea.

When you are examining your "brand," you need to look at your organization from the perspective of a potential adopter, donor, or member of the media. What you say is less important than what they perceive.

What is the first thing people think of when your organization's name is mentioned? What is the single thing that differentiates your organization from others? You need to pick one mantra, approach, or idea that no one else is using in your community.

Maybe you're the only golden retriever rescue in Tikaville. Maybe you save only animals that are over the age of ten (the gray muzzle crowd). Whatever you decide is your unique "thing," you need to put it out there consistently.

When you present your brand, you also want to make a good impression across all the media you use. For example, what impression do people get when they visit your Web site? Do they think "professional, organized, doing great work" because of the easy-to-read design and clear copy? Or do visitors think, "don't care, can't spell, and must be color-blind" because of the flashing animation, cheesy graphics, and typos?

First impressions matter. Make yours a good one

Develop Your Message

Before you begin designing your Web site or working on publicity materials and tactics, you need to think about your overall message.

You need to ask yourself:

• Why would a reporter cover you?

• What makes your group special?

• What makes your group different?

People need a quick idea or message about who you are that they can understand in less than two seconds—the simpler, the better. For example:

• Do you only rescue small dogs?

• Do you exclusively work with a particular breed?

• Are you the only ferret rescue in the Southwest?

Your message needs to be different from that of other animal groups, so people will remember who you are.

Never assume that "everyone knows" who you are and what your organization does. In many communities, animal-related charities struggle because they are being confused with other organizations. This problem happens far more frequently than people think!

In fact, here in my small community, a non-profit finally closed after 20 years of struggle, partly because of confusion about its name. The organization was called the Bonner Humane Society. For 20 years, nearly everyone thought it was the animal shelter because it included the words "humane society." It never was a shelter; it was a low-cost spay/neuter clinic.

The actual animal shelter has existed for at least 15 years; Bonner Humane should have changed its name when the shelter opened. It would have avoided a lot of aggravation and confusion in the long run (and the clinic might still exist today).

When I volunteered at the clinic, I took phone calls every single day from people wanting to bring in stray animals. I had to direct them to the animal shelter. Even the newspaper article reporting the closure of the spay/neuter clinic confused people and comments on the online version of the article indicated that people thought the *animal shelter* was closing.

A large estate donation went into litigation because it was hard to tell if the donor meant the animal shelter or the spay/neuter clinic. Countless hours were wasted because the spay/neuter clinic's board was too stubborn to change a name that obviously wasn't working. Don't let this type of thing happen to you!

Here's another example from my incredibly low-population density area. In an area with maybe 100,000 people, two groups have the words Second Chance in their organization name. One group is south of me and one is north. There's also a group called Caring People for Animals that is inevitably confused with Concerned People for Animals.

The moral of these stories is that you need to pay attention to other groups, their events, and their messaging. Do everything possible to differentiate your group from others. Being confused with another organization will make your publicity efforts a thousand times more difficult than they need to be.

As you create your materials, don't forget the facts, too. Reporters love statistics, anecdotes, and little factoids they can throw into their articles. How many animals did you adopt? How old are they? What's the oddest, most distant, or most complex adoption you've done? Did you drive a dog across the country to his new home? Any compelling facts or examples that illustrate what you do are great to include in your press materials and Web site.

Understand Web Site Basics

I'm going to lay it on the line here. Many rescue groups have terrible Web sites. A Web site is supposed to make your organization look professional, explain why people should adopt their next family pet from you, and showcase those pets to their best advantage.

In fact, you can think of your Web site as your storefront, business card, and most significant marketing piece, all rolled into one. The way your Web site affects your visitors is essential to your success. Don't forget that those visitors could be potential adopters, donors, and volunteers.

The saying "if you build it, they will come" does not apply to Web sites. Granted, over time (a long time), the search engines may eventually take note of your pages and index them, but you can't rely on that for getting visitors. The Web is more like a wilderness than a mall. No one will find you if you don't put up signs that point the way.

Most people underestimate the amount of effort it takes to properly promote a Web site for their organization. Remember that setting up a Web site is a big investment of time, dollars, or both; failing to promote it wastes that investment. Since you will be using your Web site to help promote your cause and your animals, promotion is critical.

You want your site to give your visitors a memorable experience so they'll return time and time again. Here are five keys to creating a Web site that works.

Key #1 - Make your Web site interactive.

Because the Internet continues to grow and evolve, it's important to create a community around your rescue group. See what you can do to turn your Web site into a resource. To accomplish this you'll want to engage your visitors as much as possible. You can provide engagement in number of ways:

- Provide a forum where people can ask pet-related questions, or link to a Facebook page or group where people can interact with you.

- Post surveys or polls. ("How much does your cat sleep?")

- Enable visitors and customers to comment, review, or rank things on your site. For example you could have a "write the photo caption" section. Or a multiple-choice "What is Fluffy thinking?" question with five possible answers. Or you could ask people to rate your pet photos on a scale of one to ten, where one is "get a new photographer" and ten is "cutest photo ever!"

- Set up a blog and encourage comments and feedback from visitors.

- Host contests and sweepstakes. Many rescues have a photo or essay contest, so adopters can win prizes when they showcase their animals' success story.

- Publish video and audio content, as well as written content. This gives visitors another way to see the personalities of your animals in action.

Key #2 - Make sure your Web site provides value.

People go online for a number of reasons; they go online to research a potential purchase, to seek solutions for a problem they're having, or to be entertained. If your Web site provides all three—products (or in this case adoptable animals), information, and entertainment—you're in great shape! Your content can provide both information and entertainment, and when written well, can even inspire adoptions, donations, or purchases (if you have a store). Here are a few ideas to provide value for your visitors and prospective customers:

- How-to articles, videos, and audio ("How to teach your dog to sit.")

- Tips articles, videos, and audio ("Ten tips for keeping your dog flea-free this summer.")

- Adoption stories ("Rover goes from starving stray to couch potato at his new forever home!")

- Workbooks and reports (Vaccination record books or a post-adoption handbook)

- Interviews with experts (Find a vet or behaviorist who is willing to answer the tough questions.)

- Product reviews ("Acme Dog Beds: Sure they sound like a good idea, but they don't hold up over time.")

Key #3 - Make sure your Web site is easy to navigate.

It takes a visitor somewhere between one and ten seconds to make a decision about whether they're going to stay on your Web site or click away from it. If your site is laid out nicely, with information about your organization, your services, prices, FAQs, and other content that's easy to find, people are more likely to hang out. The longer they stay on your site, the more likely they are to interact with you or return again.

To make your site easy to navigate, consider:

- Keeping your site simple.

- Keep your pages uniform, with the same options and appearance.

- If you have a lot of content, great! Use drop-down menus and organize your content by topic for easier access.

- Offer a search function so users can search for information, services, or topics quickly and easily.

- Provide a way for users to easily go back to previous pages. If every page has the same options and menus, including the ability to quickly return to the home page, a visitor will always be able to find what she needs.

- Test your Web site's appearance on different browsers to make sure every visitor has a good experience.

Key #4 - Make your Web site easy on the eyes.

Have you ever visited a Web site and found the text so small or the colors so incompatible that you couldn't read a word? Readability is critical to an engaging Web site. Make sure:

- Your colors are harmonious and not jarring or irritating
- Your graphics aren't distracting
- Formatting like underlining, bold, and italics is kept to a minimum.
- Spacing between sentences and paragraphs is adequate
- Font size is large enough for people to read and font style is easy to read

Key #5 - Give them a soft sell.

People don't visit a site to be sold to. Yes, you want people to adopt from you, but people are wary of anything that smacks of hard-sell tactics. Instead of hitting Web site visitors with a bunch of sob stories about how much you need money to keep the doors open, you should provide information, solve their pet problems, and show them the joys of pet ownership. They'll be much more receptive and appreciative.

Creating an effective Web site requires a structured approach and a desire to create the best experience possible for your visitors. Once you've created your Web site, consider testing it and asking associates, friends, and family for their opinions.

Start a Blog

Many rescues include a blog as part of their Web site to increase interactivity, or use a blog *as* their Web site.

Unfortunately, many people say they want to start a blog, but then never "get around to it." The reasons people avoid setting up a blog stem from two primary fears. The first is worrying what to write about. Fortunately, among your volunteers, you probably can find a writer or aspiring writer. However, writer or not, the second fear is fear of technology.

If you don't understand "how" a blog can be incorporated into a Web site, this one issue can become a hurdle that prevents you from moving forward. Having a blog can help bring a lot more visitors to your site, so don't let this stumbling block stop you. It's not difficult to understand.

You often can tell how a blog is set up by looking at the address bar in your browser. A blog address (URL) might appear in three basic ways, which indicate three possible ways of setting up a blog.

1. **Hosted**. Sometimes you'll see a blog that starts with the blog name right after the http://MyBlog followed by a dot, then typepad.com, wordpress.com or blogspot.com. Because of the structure of the address, you can tell it's a "hosted" blog. Hosted or Web-based blogs are located on a server somewhere that you log into. The blog is stored (or "hosted") on the blog company servers (such as Typepad), not on your own site. If that is the case, you'd go to Typepad.com and sign up. Blogger is another option. It's owned by Google and again, you'd go online, log into their server, set up the blog layout, and post your entries. Your blog address (URL) will be something like http://myblog.blogspot.com.

2. **As a part of another site**. My company blog is http://blog.logicalexpressions.com. My main Web site is www.LogicalExpressions.com. The blog is simply a folder where the blog software has been installed (the blog.logicalexpressions.com subdomain is pointed to the folder). The Small Publishers Artists and Writer's Network (SPAWN) blog is the same way. In that case, it's http://www.spawn.org/blog (the /blog part indicates that the blog is just a folder that's part of a larger site).

3. **The entire site**. In this case, the blog *is* the site. For example, www.copyblogger.com is a blog that makes up the entire Web site. The blog software is installed on their server in the main ("root") folder instead of a subfolder, and the domain points to that location. You also can point a domain to a hosted blog, as my husband did with www.LogicalHalf.com. His blog is hosted by Blogger.com, but it's more difficult to tell because he pointed a domain to it.

Each blogging option has pros and cons. The choice you make depends on the marketing goals for your blog and how much control you want over the design. Understanding the technology is actually less important than figuring out the goals for your Web site.

When you want your blog to be part of another site or if you want complete control of the customization, you need to load the blog software onto the Web server where your Web site is hosted. This option is more complicated than simply signing up for a hosted blog. Although many hosting companies offer "one-click" WordPress installation, if you hate or fear technology, setting up blog software is not a trivial exercise.

With the software approach, you generally have more freedom to design the look of your blog. Most blogs place your text within a design template. To change how the blog looks, you have to modify the underlying template. In the blogging world, these designs are often called "skins" or "themes." You can do a search and find literally thousands of themes that can be used with the various blogging software products. Just type in the name of the software and the word "skins," "templates," or "themes," and look around. However, customizing the look of your blog template requires reading the instructions and often involves knowing at least a little bit of HTML (the coding language of Web pages).

Customizing the design of a non-hosted blog is even less trivial than getting it set up in the first place. Even though countless low- or no-cost templates exist for blogs, they seldom are exactly what you want. In fact, a company called www. MyShelterSite.com offers a blog-based Web site that has been customized specifically for animal shelters and rescue groups. If you don't have a Web site already and like the idea of a site you can update yourself, it can be a good option. The service is quite limited in some ways however, so check the fine print to make sure it will do everything you need.

If you want your blog to match an existing Web site, you will have to hire a designer to customize the site for you. This generally costs some money, but it's worth it if your Web site is going to be a big part of how you get the word out about your organization.

Once the blog is set up, adding new entries is easy. You log into your blog and click the link for adding a new post. Type the subject in the first field and then add your peerless prose. Most blogs have a toolbar with buttons, so you can format your text and add links or pictures. You'll need to consult the help to find out exactly how these features work with your blog software. Once you get the hang of it, you'll find it's easy to share your thoughts with the online world. A blog can be a great promotional tool, but only if you decide to be consistent about it.

Don't let technology hold you back. If you would like to use a blog as part of your marketing and publicity tactics, learn the basics. Once a blog is set up, it's extremely easy to use, and is a great way to showcase all your activities!

Search Engine Optimization

Search engines may be the first thing you think of when we talk about Web site promotion. But are they really the best way to promote your site? The answer is maybe. Search engines are the bane and blessing of the Web experience. Although search engines index hundreds of millions of Web pages, it can still be a real challenge to locate the Web page that actually has the information you need.

The Web is cluttered with millions of Web sites and trillions of pages. Statistics show that 97% of people do not look beyond the first page of search results, so the competition for those first ten spots on the search engine results page is fierce.

Unless someone is looking specifically for your organization or something unique to your Web site, you may end up on page six or 6,000 of the search results. If you are hoping to be found using a competitive search term, it's even less likely that people will find your site through a search engine.

Getting your pages placed well in the search is a challenge. Each search engine has different rules regarding submitting pages and the rules change frequently. Your pages will fall and rise in the ranking, seemingly for no reason.

If you have your heart set on ranking high in the search engines, make sure you learn everything you can about search engine optimization (SEO). You don't want to fall for the pitch of some company that promises a "Top-10 Ranking Guaranteed!" No one can guarantee a top ranking in any search engine—at least not for all relevant searches, and certainly not permanently. Most SEO comes down to a few simple techniques. If you supply the search engines with well written content and clean HTML code, you give the search engines what they want.

Be aware that some search engines let you submit only your home page, while others allow you to submit any page you want to be indexed. Still others employ spiders, which are automated programs that can scan your entire site by following the links between pages. You must follow the submission rules for each search engine. If you don't, you may be excluded from that search engine permanently.

Quick SEO Primer

To ensure your site can be found using a search engine like Google, you need to think about search engine optimization. Getting people to your Web site (aka "traffic") is a key to your success. The more people who visit your site, the more likely it is they'll interact with you in some way, such as donating or adopting an animal.

You can do a number of things to increase the traffic to your site.

1. Understand tags.
2. Post good content.
3. Get quality links to your site.
4. Be social.

Tags You Need to Know

Title tags: Every Web page has a few "tags" that search engines look at to figure out what the page is about. The title tag is the text that appears at the top of your browser window. Make sure the title tag on each page includes keywords people might use to search for that page. If your site is a blog, you'll see a field for the title. If you are editing the HTML, a title tag looks like this: <title>My title tag with good keywords.</title>. Try to keep your title tags to less than 90 characters.

Heading tags: Search engines also look at "heading tags," which are exactly what they sound like. If you have subheads in your text, you can use heading tags to make them stand out. (It's a lot like the heading tags in your word processor, with first, second, and third level headings.) In the HTML code, they look like <h1>My first level subhead</h1>, <h2>My second level subhead</h2>, <h3>My third level subhead</h3>, and so forth.

When you tag your article this way, the search engine can tell the hierarchy. Obviously, heading one is more important than heading two.

Meta tags: There are two "meta tags" you should include on the page: description and keywords. These tags are hidden from view, but provide more clues for the search engines. The description meta tag is used for the descriptive text in the search engine results. Make sure your tags are accurate and descriptive.

Alt Tags: Alt tags are used to provide a text description of a graphic. Each graphic on your Web site should have an alt tag. In addition to helping search engines, Alt tags are important for users who are using screen readers or other accessibility tools to visit your site.

Add Content

Content is the written words on your Web site. Search engines and human beings like good content and it's important to post good content regularly to get traffic and a good ranking in the search engines. Search engines have "spiders" that go around the Internet, read your content, and index it, so searchers can find it later. Without good content, the search engines have nothing to index or rank. When you give visitors and the search engines a reason to visit your site, everybody wins.

Encourage Positive Linking: Search engines like sites that have other sites linked to it. They particularly like links from popular sites that relate to your topic. People link to articles or content they like, so that's one "natural" way you can get linked. If you work with other shelters or rescues, you can also ask if they'll link to you. Every time you submit a press release to a press-release site, you'll get a link to your site.

Be Social: I'll talk about social media later in the book, but the main thing to realize is that it's important to build a community around your Web site. Social networking can be a valuable traffic-generating tool. You can use sites like Facebook and Twitter to post links to your Web site. Just create a profile and then post comments and links to your articles to see if you can generate conversations.

Content and Keywords

If you think about it, what the search engines really want is the same thing human searchers want: an accurate selection of the best sites with content that is relevant to their search. When Google launched, it became the most popular search engine virtually overnight because it did the best job of finding relevant content; its formula was unique and effective.

Of course, the scammers eventually figured out ways to skew Google search results, and Google responded with ways to identify and penalize those scams. This game continues today and is unlikely to ever end. As a Web site owner, you have two choices: you can play the scam game and be stuck in an endless cycle of tweaking your site to use the latest tricks, or you can make your site attractive to search engines by providing exactly what they want: good content. Good content is the ultimate spider bait, and it never goes out of style.

A critical element of ranking well in the search engines is having the right "keyword density." A keyword is any word or phrase that relates to the subject of your Web page. For example, if this section of this book were a Web page, some of the keywords for it might be "search engine," "optimization," "HTML," "tags," and "content."

If your Web page contains well-written content that provides useful information, it will almost certainly (and naturally) have good keyword density. Many articles have been written suggesting what the "right" percentage of keywords is, but it changes so often that it is almost useless. You've probably run across sites that read really oddly. Tricks like this sometimes work in the short term, but can cause you to be blacklisted by the search engines later.

Instead, use your keywords naturally in your writing and avoid any artificial "keyword stuffing" in your pages. Along those lines, avoid the temptation to include the names of celebrities or other irrelevant words just to try and lure visitors.

You accomplish nothing and annoy people who are looking for content relating to those keywords. Additionally, you again risk being blacklisted by the search engines that catch on to the trick.

Keep People Coming Back to Your Site

The thing that's great about online marketing, including social media, is that you can hone your message to just the people who really care about what you do. Even better, this type of online marketing doesn't have to be expensive.

Let's face it: a lot of rescues have more time than money. You may have volunteers you can task with marketing, but no cash. The good news is that with social media, you can do a lot more with less money. You don't have to buy advertising in glossy magazines or put up billboards. Instead, you can use online marketing techniques that help build interest and trust in your organization over time.

The biggest thing animal rescues have going for them is—you guessed it—the animals themselves! Those adorable furry faces are your best marketing ambassadors, so make the most of them. Photos are a big deal online, so make sure you are making a real effort to show your animals in their best light. Take really great photos that let the personality of the animals shine.

Consider this example: the Web site ICanHasCheezbuger. com is insanely popular, yet it's just a site with captioned pictures of cats. In fact, the tagline is "Funny Pictures of Cats."

Do you have cats? Dogs? Ferrets? Critters? Yes you do!

The key is to consistently do something creative that people will want to share with their friends. Here's another example: a little while ago, nearly everyone I knew on Facebook was sharing a link from the Hyperbole and a Half blog called "Dogs Don't Understand Basic Concepts Like Moving." It's the story of a woman's move with her dogs from Montana to Oregon, which sounds boring, but it was completely hilarious to anyone who has ever owned a dog because of her descriptions of her dogs. As the owner of digestively challenged "simple" and "helper" dogs, I thought it was hysterical.

Along the same lines, on a blog called Romeo the Cat, blogger Caroline Golon chronicles her cat Romeo's "Wake-Up Tactics" of the day. In other words, she (or rather Romeo) explains the incredibly annoying technique he used to wake up his recalcitrant human. If you have a cat, perhaps you know the thrill of having Fluffy sit on your head to let you know that it's time for breakfast?

The bottom line is that if you can come up with a creative way to keep someone coming back to your Web site, over time you'll be rewarded with a community of fans. It might be photos, videos, writing, or something else. Mostly it just needs to be interesting in some way, whether it's funny, cute, unusual, or just plain helpful.

When you do something interesting and tell people about it via social media, your fans help spread the news of what you're up to through their social media connections, so your message can spread far and wide. It doesn't have to be expensive. And it might even be fun.

Take Great Photos

Using high-quality photographs is one of the easiest ways to attract the attention of the press. Even if a professional photographer isn't available, thanks to digital photography, if you take enough pictures of your animals, you eventually will get lucky and get some good photos you can use on your Web site or with your press releases.

When it comes to photographing animals, the most important thing you can capture is the animal's eyes and expression. The more captivating the expression, the more appealing the photo.

Here are some dos and don'ts of pet photography:

Do NOT:

1. **Take pictures of adoptable animals behind a chain link fence** or in a cage; you can't see the animal. Even if it's easier, you aren't doing the critter any favors. You can't see the animal's face and they look like they are in jail; that's not appealing. Try to find an uncluttered location to take your pictures. Clean up any toys or other distracting elements from the background, so the photo is focused only on the animal.

2. **Use a flash.** You want to avoid "demon" eyes. The camera flash reflects off the back of the eye when the pet's pupils are dilated, and depending on the color of the pet's eyes, you can end up with red-eye or green-eye if you use a flash. To avoid this, take photos outside in natural light or in a brightly lit room with a lot of windows, so you won't need a flash. If you have to use a flash for some reason, use an external detachable flash, so it hits the eyes at an angle. Another way to diffuse the flash is to tape a piece of cheesecloth over the flash so the light isn't as harsh.

3. **Take photos in bright, harsh sunlight.** Too much light will wash out colors and detail, and depending on the angle, bright sun will cause your pet's eyes to look "squinty." A wide-eyed open expression is more appealing than a squinty-eyed tense one.

4. **Take photos from too far away**. Composition is important. To see an animal's face, you must get up close and personal with the critter, or if that's not possible, use a zoom lens. Again, the most important thing in an animal photo is the critter's expression. People can't see the animal's face if you take the photo from afar.

DO:

1. **Allow enough time** for the photo shoot and be patient. Great pet photographs often are "happy accidents" when

you happen to click the button on the camera at just the right time. You have to give the animal time to relax, so it's helpful if the animal is in a place where he or she feels comfortable. If possible (and safe), take the picture from down on the animal's eye level. If you're taking a photo of a small dog or a cat, that may mean lying on the floor.

2. **Consider the timing of the photo shoot**. If you know that the animal always takes a post-breakfast nap, consider doing the photo shoot then. Or if you have a high-energy dog, take him for a long walk before you try to photograph him. A relaxed, slightly sleepy animal is a lot easier to photograph than one who is amped up and excited. Try to be quiet and calm yourself. Animals pick up on your energy, and if you are rushed and anxious it will be reflected in the animal photos.

3. **Enlist help**. It's a lot easier to take pet photos if you have an assistant. The assistant can hold the animal (if it's small) or the animal's leash, or help you get the pet's attention, whether with food, a noise, or a toy. Some pets can get too excited about food, so be cautious with the use of too many treats.

4. **Consider background colors.** If you can, place the animal in front of a complementary color. For example, a white dog like a Samoyed looks nice on a cool blue background (see the cover photo of this book.) And just as most redheaded humans often wear green, Irish setters or golden retrievers look nice when photographed in front of a green background. If you're photographing a black dog, you may want to put him in front of a lighter color. If you are photographing a cat, you can simulate a "backdrop" by placing the cat in the lap of a person wearing shirt or smock of a complementary color. When you take a close-up photo, the cloth will look like a background color and not a smock.

5. **Fill the frame.** The focus of the photograph is the animal, so you want to see the eyes. Try taking photos from eye-level and experiment with photos taken from just above eye level or just below. The old saying that the "eyes are the window to the soul" is particularly true for animals. You can read a lot from the expression in a pet's eyes.

6. **Find natural ways to keep the animal still**. Some dogs will hesitate just before taking a treat. Or if you put a cat on a kitty tree, many will hesitate for a few moments before leaping down. If you can capture that moment of stillness, often you'll get a great shot.

As you know, every animal has a personality. Great pet photos capture that essence and show what makes the animal special. When you look at a critter photo and it simply makes you smile, you know you have a winner.

Create an Online Media Room

The media can help you get your message out to a lot of people, but before you approach the media or the media knocks on your door, you should gather some information. This information package is often referred to as a press kit.

Ideally, you should have information about your organization ready in a form that is easily accessible to a journalist. If you can make a reporter's job easier, it might be that little extra push that puts your name in the story instead of someone else's.

These days, a press kit doesn't have to be a fancy folder filled with dozens of pieces of paper. In fact, because most reporters rely so heavily on online communication, an online press kit is a better way to offer information about your organization.

Although they may vary to some degree, your online press kit should include the following items:

1. **Summary information** about your organization. What is your mission?

2. **Information about the main people involved**, such as your board of directors or your media spokesperson. Include complete bios and credentials.

3. **Suggested interview questions** or article ideas. Remember, the goal of any online media kit is to make a reporter's job easier. If someone wants to do an interview with you, it's a lot easier if you provide the questions. Reporters are busy, so if you help them, sometimes they'll opt to write about you instead of someone else.

4. **High-resolution images** (300 dpi). Be sure to include images of your animals, your facility (if you have one), and photos related to events or information in your press releases. If you don't know how to create a press-quality image, get help from a graphic designer.

5. **Media mentions and reviews.** If you have been written up before, be sure to put links on your Web site or excerpts/quotes from articles. If you have done radio or TV interviews, see if you can get a copy of the audio or video files for your site. Sometimes you can link to the media on other sites like YouTube.

6. **A list of all the press releases** you have done, in reverse chronological order.

If you do any live or virtual events (such as a podcast), include a calendar with those event dates and links to the relevant press releases in your list.

Many people also create a PDF version of their press kit, which they can e-mail to reporters. However, please be aware that many people do not appreciate receiving this type of attachment, so send it only to reporters who specifically ask for it.

An online press kit can be a key marketing element, so give it the attention it deserves. You might just be rewarded with more media exposure.

Learn the Anatomy of a Press Release

Now it's time to get into the nitty-gritty of press releases. Some people get bogged down worrying about the format, but it's really simple. Mostly, you need to make sure that you get all the facts into the release. As someone who worked at a magazine and read thousands of press releases, I can tell you that it's surprising (and depressing) how many press releases omit basic information!

Here are the things you need to have ready:

1. **The release date**. If your press release can be used in the media immediately, put "For Immediate Release" at the top of the press release. If the information can't be published before a certain date, write "For Release" and the date and time, such as "For Release January 1, 2012, 1:00 p.m. Pacific."

2. **The contact information** for the person who should receive inquiries from reporters. For example, if someone on your board of directors is in charge of your publicity, make her the contact. Be sure you include that person's name, phone number, and e-mail address.

3. **An attention-getting headline.** Getting attention is probably the most difficult thing to do, so in the next

section I will go into detail on how to create a headline that gets noticed.

4. **An attention-getting opener** (often called the lead). What is the big idea of this story? Explain it concisely in one or two sentences.

5. **The body of the release**. In this section, you need to cover the classic five Ws and the H. In other words, the who, what, when, where, why, and how of the story. You want to include as much as possible in the first paragraph. Again, a lot of reporters aren't going to read beyond the first paragraph (and maybe even not beyond the first sentence), so you want to get everything out there quickly.

If it makes sense in the context of the story, you can include quotes from members of your organization. Put this in after the lead and the five Ws and the H. Releases are cut from the bottom, so make sure the story can work even if quotes are cut. Make sure the quotes are useful, relevant, and actually add something that's not covered elsewhere in the release.

Finally, here's a writing tip for you. After you've written your release, you'll probably be so excited that you'll want to send it out immediately.

Don't.

Wait until the next day and look it over again. Fix any problems and then get someone else to read it. You or your fellow reader may discover that you've left out something important. When you write something, you get so close to it that it's easy to overlook the obvious. Make sure you allow the extra time for review.

Attention-Getting Headlines

The headline may be the most important part of your press release. Without a good headline, your information is destined to hit the round file.

You have only a few seconds to capture your reader's attention. Creating a compelling headline has been a big part of copywriting and advertising forever, but savvy publicity seekers have used a lot of the same advice to get their press releases noticed.

Emotion is the key to a powerful headline that gets read. If you can tap into a strong emotion in the headline, the reader is more likely to read on to the first paragraph.

For example:

"A 10-Minute System that Helps You Discover Your Inner Dog-Training Genius" taps into a reader's curiosity.

A number of primary emotions relate to:

1. Attractiveness
2. Sex
3. Confidence
4. Energy
5. Money
6. Being special (pampering)
7. Community/belonging
8. Feeling in control
9. Pride
10. Respect
11. Safety

When you're writing headlines, it's also important to use the active tense (as opposed to the passive tense). Language that conveys movement and activity commands attention.

For example, "Shelter Adopts Four Cats" is a somewhat bland headline. It doesn't include emotion or inspire much interest. However, a headline like "Shelter Conquers Negative Perception of Black Cats with New Promotion and Adopts Homeless Family of Four Felines in First 15 Minutes" is more compelling.

The reason it's better is because "conquer" is an interesting and active verb. The specifics in the headline also make it more interesting, particularly to anyone who loves cats. When you understand your audience, you realize that the word "family" resonates with cat lovers because they view their feline friends as part of their family. The more you can tie into the audience's emotions, the more successful the headline will be.

Many experts suggest writing multiple headlines and then picking the best of the bunch. The headline is probably the most important part of your press release, so it's worth it to spend some time crafting a good one.

Publicity in Action

Example Release: Appraise for Strays

FOR IMMEDIATE RELEASE

Contact: Antique Market xxx-xxx-xxxx or
                Sandy Smith xxx-xxx-xxxx

Appraise for Strays Fund-Raiser for Animal Shelter To Be Held on April 15

The Antique and Country Market at Fifth and Cedar is again hosting the "Appraise for Strays" antique and collectible appraisal show on Saturday, April 15 from 11:00 a.m. to 4:00 p.m. At the event, people can learn more about their treasures and their estimated value from knowledgeable collectors. The event is much like the antique appraisal "road shows" on television, except it has the added benefit that it helps raise money for the Animal Shelter. Everyone is welcome to bring antique items for evaluation. Each item costs $2 (or 3 for $5) to evaluate. All of the money from the appraisal fees is donated to the Animal Shelter to help care for homeless and unwanted animals in our community.

Knowledgeable antique collectors and dealers are donating their time to share their expertise and excitement about the world of antique collecting. People will be on hand who are well-versed in antique clocks, watches, hunting and fishing collectibles, military memorabilia, coins, antique pattern glass, silver, Depression glass, pottery, dolls, the general line of antiques and collectibles, and more.

Almost everyone has heirlooms or collectibles that have been handed down from generation to generation. This Appraise for Strays fund-raiser is a great opportunity to find out more about their value. The appraisals are intended to be used only as a guide to approximate values. Prices may vary in other parts of the country, and the members of the panel are not necessarily licensed appraisers. The event will be informal with lots of audience participation and is a great opportunity to meet people who can help you evaluate all those mystery items lurking in your closet or attic.

###

Example Follow-Up Release

FOR IMMEDIATE RELEASE

Contact: Antique Market xxx-xxx-xxxx or

Sandy Smith xxx-xxx-xxxx

Appraise for Strays A Paw-tastic Success!

Last Saturday everyone had the opportunity to forget about taxes for a few hours. At the Antique and Country Market, 100 people brought in more than 250 items to be examined by knowledgeable collectors and dealers. Twelve people at five tables were delighted with the collection of watches, guns, dolls, jewelry, china, glass, books, military memorabilia, and small furniture items that people brought in for them to look at. The event earned $502, which will be used to help care for the animals at the Animal Shelter.

Everyone was more than willing to share a story. For example, Jan Davis brought in a watch and a silver cigarette case that belonged to her father, Wes Kingdon, who was a professional baseball player in the early '30s. A few other highlights included a bisque-headed composition baby doll with original clothes that was valued in the $2,000 range. Another Madam Alexander doll was valued in the $1,000-$1,500 range, and a carnival glass hatpin holder had an estimated value of around $200.

Sandy Smith, a shelter volunteer who helped out at the event, said, "We hope to do this again late this summer, so people can bring bigger items. Plus we want to have a 'bragging table' where people can sit and show and tell other folks about their items while they wait for a particular person to look at their stuff. The shelter also would like to extend a huge thank-you to all the folks at the Antique Market for making this event such a great success."

Where to Send Your Release

Once you have your press release written, it's time to get it out into the world. Where you send it depends a lot on the story.

If you are sending a press release about a local event, don't bother sending it to national media; it's a waste of your time and potentially money. (Some national press release distribution services are extremely expensive!)

Yes, I know, everyone wants to get on "Oprah" or "Good Morning America," but you need to start small. Start with smaller media and work up to bigger outlets. For example, start with the local freebie rag. Move up to the weekly paper, then the daily paper, then regional, and even national.

It's easy to create a list of local media by spending some time surfing their Web sites. It can be most effective and certainly less expensive to create and maintain your own media database, particularly if you live in a small town without many media outlets.

You can find a lot of contact information in the public library and online. At your library, you'll find media directories from companies such as Bacon, Burrelle, Gale, and Gebbie Press. Generally these directories are located in the reference section, so you can't check them out, but you can make copies of relevant sections, so you can add the information to your media list.

Don't forget to add local "events" Web sites and even college or high school newspapers to your media list. When you're at the grocery store or out and about your town, look for racks of "free newspapers." Grab a copy of anything that looks interesting and add the contact information (from the masthead) to your list.

A number of Web sites have information about newspapers. For example, the US Newspaper Links (USNPL) site http://www.usnpl.com/ lets you search for newspapers and get their addresses. If you don't want to spend a lot of time copying and pasting, you can buy the contact information in Word or Excel format for single states, or the entire US. The site also has somewhat more limited information on radio stations, TV stations, and colleges.

Another less comprehensive Web site with newspaper contact information is the news section of 50States.com: http://www.50states.com/news/. When you click your state, you get a list of links to all the Web sites for the various news outlets.

Online Distribution

In addition to local media, you can get wider exposure for your release online by submitting it through various online distribution services. When you do this, it's actually fairly unlikely you'll get any major media "hits," so don't get your hopes up too high.

When it comes to the paid sites, be aware that spending more money does not necessarily guarantee better distribution. You need to read the fine print carefully, and journalists are extremely overworked. In many cases, no human will even look at your release, no matter how much you spent. If something big happens in the world the day your release goes out, it will be ignored.

With all that said, one of the side effects of using online press release distribution is getting an incoming link to your Web site. And all those incoming links are great for your search engine positioning.

Some online distribution services are free, in the hope that you'll upgrade to one of their paid add-on services. If you do a search, you'll find dozens of free PR distribution sites online, but here are a few to get started:

- www.pressmethod.com
- www.PR.com
- www.mediasyndicate.com
- www.prlog.org
- www.i-newswire.com
- www.PRLeap.com

Bear in mind that search engines consider incoming links from "high-authority" sites more valuable, so getting your press release on these free PR sites isn't likely to make a huge difference.

Paid PR distribution sites are syndicated to high-authority sites, so submitting to a paid service can have value in the long run; however, you need to really think about whether your story has national appeal. If you have a great story and enough of a budget to submit your release to paid services, here's a list of some of the popular ones:

- www.PRWeb.com
- www.BusinessWire.com
- www.PRNewswire.com
- www.cision.com
- www.majon.com
- www.Send2Press.com

Write Letters and Tip Sheets

You can go way beyond a standard press release to get your name in the media more frequently. In addition to the traditional "newsy" press release, you have other options for getting your name in the media. One easy thing to do is to simply send letters to the editor. If there's an animal-related story, send a letter commenting on it.

Tip sheets are another often-underutilized technique. A tip sheet is just a news release that has a list of tips or advice. You've probably seen countless articles that are based on tip sheets without even realizing it. Have you ever seen a little newspaper blurb that is something along the lines of "7 Ways to Keep Your Dog Safe During the Summer"? That article probably came from a tip sheet release someone sent in. The reason tip sheets work is that they make great "filler" material for those times when the journalist or publisher realizes "Oops, we need something for this space...what do we have?"

Sometimes a reporter or editor will use a tip sheet almost verbatim. Other times your release might entice a reporter or producer to write a longer feature article or interview you about the topic. The great thing about the tips is that they are often "evergreen," which means that even if it doesn't get picked up immediately, you may get a welcome surprise when a reporter desperate to fill some column inches calls you about a tip sheet you sent out months ago.

To create a tip sheet, use the standard press release format, but instead of focusing on the five Ws and H, the body of the release is your tips. As with a press release, you want a compelling headline that captures attention.

One great way to find headlines that work is to leaf through the magazines at the checkout stand in the grocery store. If you pick up a magazine like *Cosmo*, you'll notice many articles that start "7 Ways..." "5 Tips for..." "6 Hints..." and so on. You can model your headlines on these proven formulas that have sold magazines at the checkout aisle for years.

In your first paragraph, explain why the tips are important, the problem they solve, and the credentials of the expert offering the helpful solution. The tips should be in numbered or bulleted format so they are easy to read quickly. The end of the release should include your contact information.

Publicity in Action

Example Tip Sheet

Here's a tip sheet I wrote to promote my books *Happy Hound* and *Happy Tabby*. Obviously, this tip sheet was promoting me as an expert because I wrote the books. If you work at a shelter or rescue, the tips could be from your executive director or board president.

Complete Cleaning Is No Accident: Cleaning Tips for Pet Owners to Prevent Repeat Offenses

SANDPOINT, Idaho - "Accidents" are a fact of life for pet owners, and how well the soiled area is cleaned affects whether or not the animal uses that spot for his personal toilet again. The author of two books on adopted pet care, Susan Daffron of Logical Expressions, Inc., offers a few cleanup tips based on her books *Happy Hound: Develop a Great Relationship with Your Adopted Dog or Puppy* (ISBN: 978-0-9749245-2-6; LCCN-2006909898) and *Happy Tabby: Develop a Great Relationship with Your Adopted Cat or Kitten* (ISBN: 978-0-9749245-3-3; LCCN-2007906436).

1. Get up close and personal with the carpet. Pets have a vastly more sensitive sense of smell than humans. Even if a spot seems clean, a pet still knows that's where he left his "scent." If the smell is noticeable, the pet certainly can detect it and will return to the same spot. Use your nose and eyes to find every problem area.

2. Seek out old stains. A black-light bulb can reveal old urine stains. Turn out all the lights in the room and use the black light to identify long-standing problem areas.

3. Remove odors completely. To clean the areas so the odors are really gone, use an enzymatic cleaner and follow the instructions on the bottle carefully. These cleaners actually neutralize the odor, as opposed to just covering them up.

4. Clean up new accidents as soon as they happen. If an accident has just occurred, soak up as much of the urine/liquid as possible with a folded towel or a stack of paper towels. Stand or press on this pad until the area is barely damp. Then use the enzymatic cleaner on the spot. Rinse the area with cool water and blot with a towel.

5. Avoid using cleaning chemicals that don't eliminate odor. Common cleaning agents such as ammonia or vinegar don't eliminate odor completely. Using other strong chemicals may also decrease the effectiveness of the enzymatic cleaner.

Avoid using steam cleaners to remove urine, because the heat can permanently set the stain.

Once the house is thoroughly cleaned, begin retraining your pet. Without the smells to distract him, it will be easier for him to do the right thing. And that's good news for your carpet!

For more information about *Happy Hound*, visit http://www.HappyHoundBook.com. *Happy Tabby* information is at http://www.HappyTabbyBook.com, and information on other products is available at www.logicalexpressions.com.

\###

Media Contact:

Susan Daffron, President of Logical Expressions, Inc.

+1-208-265-6147

sdaffron@logicalexpressions.com

Attract Attention

Publicity can be one of the best ways to get the word out about your organization. However, you can't write a press release, sit back, and wait for the interviews to roll in. Rescue groups that do that are often disappointed; they write a press release and then wonder why nothing happens.

Unfortunately, getting media coverage often requires more than just a press release. You are competing for coverage with an unbelievable number of other releases every single day. You won't score an interview, article, or mention in the media just because you think your group is great or because you sent out one press release.

The key to getting coverage is by giving the media what they really want: news their audience cares about. In other words, the easier you can make a reporter or producer's job, the more likely you are to get the press to mention your organization. Here are a few tips to think about:

1. **Keep up with news on your topic.** News is not about things that are unchanged or that didn't happen. In other words, you don't see articles with headlines like "No Freeway Accidents Today." One tried and true way to get noticed by the press is to link your story to current events. Newsworthy topics recount events, changes, or other things that affect people's lives. An easy way to keep

up with news on your topic is to create a Google alert for specific terms or phrases. Go to http://news.google.com, click the News Alerts link and follow the steps.

2. **Tell a story.** The terms "pitch" or "news hook" just refer to a story idea. As noted, reporters are busy. If you can do the reporter's job for him, you might just get coverage. Think of a pitch as if it were a really short, short story. You will need to understand the audience for the story and how it will appeal to their needs. Obviously the story you would tell for a pet products industry newsletter would be different from one for a women's magazine. First find the media outlets and reporters you want to target, then craft a short, pithy story that makes the reporter think, "Wow, that would be a great article!" Unlike a press release, which announces news or events, this letter can be more personal and addressed to a specific reporter or writer.

It's all about making the reporter's job easy. Put your high-resolution photos online, so you can give the reporter just a link. Most people won't open unsolicited attachments, so don't send a bunch of stuff until you are asked, because odds are good it will become a victim of the Delete key.

Always remember that you are the expert and the media needs you. If you are asked to do an interview, write out your points in advance, so you don't fumble around trying to find your topic again. If you are prepared and confident, you may be rewarded with great publicity that can dramatically affect the public's perception of your rescue group. And the reporter is more like to return to you for similar information in the future.

Hooks are for Fish; Tell Stories

When people talk about "pitching" the media or media "hooks," it sounds complicated, but it's really not. A publicity guru once said that hooks are for hanging pictures. Don't worry about having a "hook." What you need is a story.

In fact, publicist Maggie Jessup told me recently that the main reason her press releases are picked up is that they read like a story. Before she became a publicist, she was a journalist for large newspapers. She wrote literally dozens of stories some days, and she pointed out that the more a press release reads like a final news story, the more likely it will be run.

Reporters like easy. They don't know anything about you, your organization, or whatever you're trying to promote. You may think that what you're saying is obvious, but it's probably new to them. Don't take anything for granted and don't make a reporter work to get information.

The main thing to remember is that people remember stories, not facts.

Think about it. When you were in school, memorizing facts about history was boring, but everyone knows the story of Paul Revere's ride or the Boston Tea Party. You may not know the date, but you know the story. The more you can wrap a "story" around what you do, the easier it is to get press.

For example, in his speeches, Mike Arms of the Helen Woodward Animal Center often shares a story about a call he got from someone who had a nine-year-old Rottweiler and six puppies. Mike sent someone to bring in the dog and the pups, so they could be put up for adoption at the center.

Every day people drop off older animals that "accidentally" have puppies. This type of thing isn't "new news" to you; it's a daily occurrence, and it was at Helen Woodward, too. According to Mike, when they got the rotties, staff members said, "Who is going to want a nine-year-old Rottweiler and six puppies?"

Mike's response was that if you say it that way, no one will. But if you say that a 63-year-old has given birth to sextuplets, the media will notice. He was right. The media were all over the story and the mom and all of her puppies were adopted into good homes.

Never underestimate the value of a good story. It makes all the difference!

Thinking Like the Media

The key to getting publicity is to learn what makes the news. Once you understand what is "newsworthy," and how to spot the "story" in what you want to say, it's much easier to get attention.

When you encounter news, whether online, in print, or on TV, consider why the story was covered in the first place. Reporters get literally hundreds or thousands of releases every day. How did the media outlet find out about the story you saw on the news? Why did they care? What caused them to select that story? Then consider if there are elements of the story you could apply to your own situation.

To give you an example, I opened Google News and did a search on dog rescue. Here are a few headlines and why I think they made the news:

1. **"Katherine Heigl and her mother have a dog-gone good time with a rescue puppy"**

   This one includes a celebrity. Has anyone famous adopted a pet from you? Get a quote and send out a press release. It's news.

2. **"Humane Society Wraps Up Large-Scale Dog Rescue"**

   This article is an event. You may be involved in saving dogs all the time, but if anything out of the ordinary happens (like a large-scale rescue), it's news.

3. **"Neglected Dog 'Ginger' Continues Recovery"**

   This article tells a story of a dog named Ginger who was a victim of animal cruelty. Never underestimate the value of telling an interesting story. That one dog's story can help a lot of other dogs get adopted, too.

4. **"Local rabbit rescue organization sees adoption spike during Easter"**

   In this case, the article is tied to a seasonal event: Easter. Every year you have countless opportunities for press. In addition to holidays like Easter, you can send a release for Spay Day USA, Adopt a Cat/Dog Day and so forth. Look online for holidays and you'll come up with a lot of opportunities for press.

5. **"Rescue group fights to keep starved dog from returning home"**

   Here we have a classic "David vs. Goliath" tale, where the rescue group is trying to fight a bureaucracy to help a dog. Any time you can add a dramatic or novel twist to a story, it's newsworthy. People respond to stories where they can root for the underdog (so to speak).

Start looking at the news with a publicist's eye and you'll realize that definite themes appear. It's not news if Jane Smith adopts a dog. But it is news if a famous celebrity adopts a dog. When you learn how to come up with story angles that showcase something different, timely, or creative, you're more likely to get more press.

Be Fast

If you've never worked at a newspaper or other media outlet, you might not realize how deadline-driven the news can be. One often-overlooked aspect of getting publicity is that you have to be available and you have to be fast.

The reality is that reporters usually have a list of people to contact about a story. If they call you, odds are good they won't leave a message. They'll just move down to the next person on the list, who will get the publicity and you won't.

Here's a simple tip: consider answering your phone.

Unfortunately, a lot of rescue groups have terrible customer service. They let a machine take their incoming calls and then return messages "sometime." That type of poor customer service certainly doesn't help your adoption statistics, and it certainly won't help you get publicity.

Along the same lines, if you get an e-mail from a reporter, you should answer it now. Not two days from now. Obviously, you can't be at your computer 24/7, so realistically, sometimes publicity can be partly about luck. If you're in the right place at the right time, you can get lucky.

Here's a real example. One Sunday I was checking my e-mail. A contact form e-mail arrived from a reporter from Reuters who was looking for comments that related to an article I had written. He provided his phone number, so I called him immediately. After I talked to him, I also replied to the original e-mail with all my contact information, so he'd have the correct spelling of my name and company.

I was rewarded with an article that included two great (and long) quotes from me as an expert. And the article was syndicated to multiple media outlets like the Los Angeles *Times*. And a blogger from *Forbes* picked up my quote out of the original Reuters article.

The moral of the story here is that you can help "make your own luck" by being available as much as you possibly can.

When you deal with members of the media, clearly time is of the essence. So is brevity. Ideally, you should be able to get your main point across to reporters in ten to fifteen seconds. Any extra time you get for an interview is a gift. The other thing to remember is that everything you say really IS "on the record."

Even if the reporter says something is "off the record," don't believe it. Information that is supposed to be "off the record" may or may not be included, so always err on the side of caution. You might think that the "official" interview is over and you're just chatting. You aren't. You're talking to a reporter and everything you say could be used. So choose your words wisely. Don't say anything you wouldn't want your Mom to know you said, or you may regret it later.

Follow-up

Most reporters will tell you that they hate follow-up calls or e-mails. They steadfastly assert that they don't want to be bothered. However, anyone who has ever tried to get publicity will tell you follow-up and tenacity can pay off. If you don't get a response from your initial contact, the person may not be interested or may simply be too busy to deal with it at that time. You don't know if you don't ask.

A reporter's life can be hectic, so if you don't hear back from someone, it may not be your fault. Follow up by e-mail or phone about once/week and try and be as polite and friendly as you can. Many people recommend following up at least seven times before giving up. Don't be a pest and also don't ask "if they got the press release." Instead, point out that you sent some information and remind them why it's a good story and why they should care. If they do say no, respect that, but nicely see if you can find out why. It may be your angle, the timing, or any one of a thousand other variables.

How To Come Up with Press Release Ideas

If you've spent some time developing a nose for news, you probably have some ideas for a press release. Remember that you don't have to stick with the obvious news items like "we're having an event."

Yes, that's news, but it's kind of a boring story. Think about the last novel you read. Why was the story interesting? Probably because there was a hero who did something interesting. Maybe there was a love interest and some conflict. Maybe the book had some funny moments too.

Can you incorporate any of those elements into the story for your release? There are a lot of heroes in rescue, so finding one would not be difficult. People do amazing things for animals every day, and conflicts and controversy run rampant in the humane world. (Often to our detriment!)

And of course, animals are funny. Some of the humor you see may not be ideal for public consumption, but some classic news stories are actually funny, like the cliché "man bites dog." If you need more examples, check out Yahoo's online "weird news."

If you're not much of a dramatic writer or can't think of anything funny, you have yet another source for press release ideas. Simply ask yourself who you help and how you help them. For example, maybe you have a special program that adopts animals to seniors. Programs like that can inspire a great "feel good" story.

The idea is to present stories to the media that don't even remotely resemble any type of advertising. Anything that smacks of sales is a huge turn-off. The media get countless releases that are really nothing more than a sales pitch, and all of those releases end up in the round file.

If you tell your story from the spirit of giving and helpfulness, you inspire trust. That trust is what brings people to your door or to donate to your cause, which is the whole reason you want publicity in the first place.

Creating a Plan and Tracking Results

There's an old saying that nothing happens without a plan, and that is true of publicity. As you've been reading along, you may have thought, "Hmm, I could write a lot of press releases." Yes, you could. And if you do, you will dramatically increase your odds of getting attention. The process doesn't have to be overwhelming if you lay out a publicity plan.

To create your plan, sit down with a calendar and your ideas. You need to know the lead times for various media. If you want your story to appear in magazines, for example, you may be surprised to learn that they need a minimum of four to six months lead time. Weekly newspapers need four to six weeks lead time and daily papers two to three weeks. Radio and TV news have lead times as short as a couple of days, but longer shows like TV specials or documentaries may require months of lead time.

With this information in mind, it's time to start adding press release dates to your calendar.

1. First, add your scheduled events to your calendar. For example, if you do a big "Fur Ball" fundraiser during the holidays and a dog walk in the summer, put those major events on your calendar. For daily and weekly newspapers,

you need to send your releases to calendar editors, metro editors, and feature editors. If the newspaper has a special "pets" section, make sure that editor is included on your list.

2. For every major event, you will need to write a minimum of three press releases.

    • An initial event announcement that explains that the event is coming and how people can help. Send out this release at least three to six weeks before the event.

    • A press release with the finalized details of event and the reasons people should attend. Send this out seven to ten days before the event.

    • A post-event release with the results of the event. Tout the success, explain how the money you raised will help the animals, and thank all the volunteers. Send this release immediately after the event.

3. If you participate in other smaller activities or events, such as a town "winter carnival," add those press releases into your calendar as well. For these smaller events, you may need just one press release.

4. Decide how many tip sheets you want to do in the year. For example, you might opt to do one per month in the months when you aren't doing a huge event. You'd add those ten releases to your calendar.

5. Optionally, do press releases for special pet-related holidays like Spay Day USA, Cat Adoption Week, Dog Adoption Week, and so forth. If you do an online search, you can find huge lists of pet-related holidays for specific dates each year. Here are few of the biggies that have been around for a while:

    • February - Spay Day USA, Prevent a Litter Month

    • April - Prevention of Cruelty to Animals Month

    • May - Be Kind to Animals Week, Dog-Bite Prevention Week

- June - Take Your Dog to Work Day, Adopt a Shelter Cat Month
- October - Adopt a Shelter Dog Month
- November - National Animal Shelter Appreciation Week

You can coordinate some of your tip sheets to correspond to major holidays, too. Don't forget that with the long lead time of magazines, you'll be sending out your holiday tip sheet in June and your Fourth of July tip sheet in March.

Measure Your Success

Once you have written and sent your press release, you need to keep track of what happens. You can't make changes to improve your publicity results unless you keep track of what happened (or didn't happen).

The reality is that you can't control the media, so not every press release is going to get picked up. The reason it isn't picked up may be that you need more practice writing interesting media-friendly releases, or the reason may be completely out of your control. I've often told the story of how I did a big direct mailing for a magazine and mailed it September 10, 2001. Needless to say, the response rate was zero. Sometimes you send out a press release and big news hits in the world that trumps everything.

Don't feel like you've "failed" at getting publicity when you don't get the response you hoped for from your publicity efforts. The main thing is to keep track of what you did, so you can keep trying and improving your results over time. Think of publicity as a marathon, not a sprint. Occasionally, people get lucky with a huge media "win" on their first try, but most people have to keep working at it over time.

In general, when you send out a release through a service, you'll start getting results online or offline within one to three days. During this time, you're most likely to receive phone calls or e-mail queries for interviews or requests for more information. Be sure to keep track of what happens.

Here are some things you should monitor:

1. **Phone calls.** How many people called you after the release came out?

2. **E-mails.** How many people e-mailed?

3. **Web site traffic.** Check your Web stats/analytics. Did your site see a spike in visitors?

4. **Click-throughs from other sites.** Check the "referrers" section of your statistics and see if anyone has clicked through from media outlets or the press-release submission sites.

5. **Web site mentions.** Set up a Google Alert so you can tell if other sites republish your release. (I explain how to set up a Google alert in the next section.)

6. **Social media or newsgroup mentions**. Has your release (or a new story related to it) been Tweeted or mentioned on Facebook? Are people talking about it in newsgroups?

7. **Stories from the release.** Obviously if you get a TV interview or big write-up in a newspaper or online, that's a big win!

8. **Increased inquiries or visits** from potential adopters or volunteers. Be sure to ask people how they heard about you. It could be a news story!

9. **Syndicated news mentions.** If you haven't paid attention to the news media, you may not realize that a lot of news stories are "syndicated," which means the same story runs on multiple sites.

Like I said, I was quoted in an article published by Reuters. This is an example of syndication; Reuters is a service that syndicates its articles to many newspapers. So my quote ended up in everything from the Los Angeles *Times* to Yahoo News.

The Associated Press (AP) is another big syndicator. (You'll be celebrating if the AP picks up your story!) If you discover that an article mentioning you has been syndicated, visit news.Google.com to see if you can track down all the papers that picked it up.

Set Up Google Alerts

Google Alerts are an easy way to monitor your online mentions. When you set up Google Alerts, it's kind of like having an online "clipping service" working for you. You set up terms that you want Google to monitor for you and when the term appears online, Google sends you an e-mail with the link that mentions your term.

The key to not getting overwhelmed with e-mail is to keep your search terms really specific. You can use the standard Google search operators to help narrow your search, such as putting a term like "golden retriever" in quotes to avoid getting results related to everything golden. Or you can combine terms, such as humane + society. You also can exclude terms, so you avoid getting results about things you aren't interested in, like "Samoyed rescue" - grooming (if you want to get results about Samoyed rescue, but avoid receiving links to pages about caring for shedding Samoyeds).

To set up a Google alert:

1. Go to www.google.com/alerts.

2. Put in your search terms. For example, if your shelter is the South Tikaville Animal Shelter, put the whole name in quotes, so you get mentions of just your shelter and not information about the entire town. (Note that you need to create a separate alert for each term.)

3. Select the type of alert to create. (Most of the time you want "everything.")

4. Decide how often you want to receive alerts.

5. Select best results or all results.

6. Type your e-mail address and create the alert.

After you start getting alerts, you may find you need to tweak your settings. If you have a Google account, you can just change the alert settings. If you don't have a Google account, you can cancel the alert and start over with a new one. Because I use my Gmail e-mail address for my alerts, it's easy to edit them later. If you have problems, you can find help for alerts here: www. google.com/support/alerts/.

Dealing with Crises

In the life of every rescue or humane group, you will undoubtedly encounter a publicity crisis. It may be a situation where an adopter is unhappy, or worse, it could be another animal group calling you names.

Right now, here in our tiny community, one animal group is trying to trash a local shelter in the media for not housing animals for their program. They've called a "community meeting" and are trying to recruit support in social media. (But they are deleting any dissenting comments...welcome to the world of social media censorship.)

As part of their smear campaign, they placed an ad in the local paper with one out-of-context sentence that implies the local shelter is being uncooperative. What isn't being mentioned is:

- Participating in the program would violate the mission of the shelter and their bylaws.
- Participating in the program would tie up a kennel because the animals can't be adopted while in the program. If a kennel is tied up, obviously another homeless animal can't use it.
- The shelter has a contractual obligation to the city and county to house their homeless pets.

Most people don't know the full story. They read the one-sided advertisement in the local paper and think, "Wow, what a bad, evil shelter!"

No one goes beyond that to ask, "Why *should* a shelter use its limited funds to feed and house animals for another program?" (The obvious logical solution to this problem is for the group slandering the shelter to simply adopt animals for their program from the shelter and then find them new homes afterward.)

Here's the worst part. Personal attacks on animal groups and the individuals working in shelters and rescues happen all the time. Facts get twisted, and horrible publicity results. This problem isn't new. I had to go on TV ten years ago to explain why an animal at the shelter I was working at could not safely be adopted and was euthanized.

No one wants to hear about killing. But a TV sound bite doesn't give you much time to explain about dog-bite liability, either. Some problems are complex and inevitably someone with an agenda will try to use the power of publicity against you.

When passions run high, misinformation is the rule. In our highly connected world, a lot of people don't let facts get in the way of their agenda. People from across the country or across the world who have never met you or visited your facility can spew inaccurate vitriol for any reason (or no reason at all).

Here's what you can do when a crisis hits:

1. Establish a basis of support in your community and proactively reach out to the media. If a reporter gets a "tip" that seems out of character for your organization, he'll be more likely to call you before running a damaging story.

2. Practice transparency. Own up to your mistakes if you make them. Explain what you plan to do to resolve problems.

3. Look for ways to make a positive contribution. Tearing down other organizations helps no one.

John Q. Public doesn't really understand the nuances of different humane groups. If they all are sniping at each other, John doesn't adopt an animal at all because "they're all bad."

It's time for people in the humane world to start acting like grown-ups. We should all be doing our part to work together to solve the problem of homeless animals. Stop trying to tear down other groups. Build up your own!

Word-of-Mouth Publicity

Some days it's difficult to stay motivated, and sometimes things can feel a little overwhelming. Maybe it seems like you're doing all these fantastic things to help the animals and nobody notices or seems to care. Maybe you've been busy busting your you-know-what for a big holiday fundraiser. Then you admit twelve puppies that need vet care, so you really need that fundraiser to work even more.

The key is to not get discouraged or sound desperate or angry. Word-of-mouth is part of publicity. People donate to great causes every day. They do it to feel good. We all know that bad things can happen. More animals always need rescuing, you'll encounter abuse, and sometimes you'll see truly terrible situations. But when you are talking to people on the phone or in person, you want to project a positive image.

People are more attracted to a rescue group if they believe it knows what it's doing and is making a positive difference in the community. When people hear about a rescue that's desperately screaming for money and constantly in crisis, it doesn't inspire confidence.

I know we all have bad days, but when you answer that phone or talk to that volunteer, consider the impact your words can have. Always do your best to project a calm, positive attitude. When you do, you'll be rewarded with better results all around!

Section 2

Publicity
Tactics

Hold a Newsworthy Event

Throughout this book I point out that you can use publicity for more than events, but hosting an event *is* a tried-and-true way to get publicity. An event by its nature is "news," and when you host some type of fundraiser, you have a great opportunity to tell the media what you are doing.

For every event you have at least three (sometimes more) opportunities for publicity:

1. **Before the event**: do a press release to announce what you are doing and when it's happening. (Remember the five Ws and the H.)

2. **During the event**: see if you can get a media outlet to cover it. Or tell a story about someone affected by the event. "Our long-time shelter resident Rover was finally adopted to a loving home. His new owners received a free vet exam, Nylabone, and microchip. Everyone is thrilled!"

3. **After the event**: do a press release describing the results and thanking everyone involved.

When it comes to the media, an "event" doesn't necessarily mean something big at a particular time, like a dog walk. It can be something much simpler or smaller, such as a letter-writing campaign or product sales. The bottom line is to always tell the media what you are doing.

Events give people opportunities to engage with your organization. Although a lot of groups focus on the fundraising aspect of events, don't underestimate the "friend-raising" element as well. By hosting various events throughout the year, you give potential donors and adopters multiple ways to get involved in your organization.

For example, some donors might be more "hands-off" and will want to just send money. Those people may respond to direct mail or an online donation opportunity. They might decide to visit your great new Web site after reading an article about it. You never know what event will spur people to take action.

Other donors want to engage with your organization on a more personal level. These people may be excited about live events like dog walks. By alerting the media and sharing the news about *all* of your events (even seemingly "small" ones), you'll see the most results. After all, different people respond to different things.

For every event, be sure to tell a "story" that grabs people's interest. Make sure you have a great headline that attracts attention. If you're doing a live event, be very sure to take a *lot* of pictures of people having a good time, or you can even create a fun video. Post the photos/videos on your Web site and in your final press release, and be sure to include a link and point out that high-resolution versions of the photos are available. You never know when a cool photo or funny video will be just the thing that capture's a reporter's attention.

The Canine Event of the Season

When I was doing publicity and fundraising work for our local shelter, we put on a huge community event, called the Bow Wow Pow Wow, at the county fairground.

Dubbed the "canine event of the season," we brought in vendors, had contests, and really did it up. Although the Bow Wow Pow Wow was an amazing "friend-raiser," the first year, it didn't make as much money as we'd hoped. However, people loved it, so we decided to do it again. By the second year, people were looking forward to it and it made more money than it had the first year. Unfortunately, the management of the shelter changed and the event was never held again. Years later, people still ask me why it went away, because no other fun "dog event" ever replaced it.

If you make a commitment to your events, you can turn them into something that people anticipate every year. Once the event has some momentum, getting publicity will be easier and easier every year. Even though it may take a few years before the event really starts to make a lot of money, make sure you keep the long-term picture in mind and remember that the publicity you generate because of the event can pay off in other ways too, such as increased adoptions or donations.

Publicity in Action

Bow Wow Pow Wow: Sample Releases

People often struggle to come up with ideas for press releases, so I'm including a couple of samples that I wrote many years ago for the Bow Wow Pow Wow. Note that you can reuse some of the information in your follow-up releases, so the first press release is probably the most difficult one to write. Also, take note of the fact that press releases don't have to be particularly long. One page (300-500 words) is plenty.

In this first release, notice how I have made sure to share the publicity joy by mentioning all the sponsors, the local radio station, the fairground and so forth. Never forget that people *love* to see their names in print.

FOR IMMEDIATE RELEASE

Contact: Susan Daffron, Animal Shelter
                Public Relations, at xxx-xxx-xxxx

Every Dog Has His Day at the Bow Wow Pow Wow

At the Animal Shelter's second annual Bow Wow Pow Wow, you'll be able to support your local animal shelter, shake the paw of a local canine hero, and show off your best friend, all in one fun-filled afternoon. The Bow Wow Pow Wow will be held on September 25 from 11:00 a.m. to 4:00 p.m. at the County Fairground. Billed as THE canine social event of the year, the event features lots of fun contests, prizes, and demonstrations. All proceeds from the Bow Wow Pow Wow benefit the spay/neuter cost-assistance program at the shelter, which to date has given out more than $8,000 worth of coupons to help area pet owners get their dogs and cats "fixed."

All well-behaved dogs and their families are invited to attend. Every dog must be accompanied by an adult and be under control at all times (in other words, all dogs must have humans attached to the end of their leash). Dogs will have fire hydrants and water available for their comfort and humans will have food and beverages available for their comfort, too. Owners should make sure that their dogs' vaccinations are up to date before attending.

The festivities start at 11:00 a.m. with canine competitions, including the Cute Miss contest for females and the Handsome Hunk contest for males. Dogs can show off their special gifts at the Talent Show and other contests such as Best Tail Wagger, Most Mysterious Heritage, Best Begging Face, and the Dog/

Owner Look-Alike. The top three dogs in each category receive ribbons, applause, and the adulation of their canine peers. KPND is doing a live outside broadcast of the event courtesy of Thorne Research Veterinary Products and Coldwater Creek, so a deejay will keep everyone informed of the ongoing demonstrations and contests throughout the day.

This year the Bow Wow Pow Wow is sponsored by local Sandpoint veterinary clinics Animal Medical Care, Bonner Animal Hospital, North Idaho Animal Hospital, and Pend Oreille Veterinary Clinic. Veterinary information booths and pet care advice will be available along with a special visit from Ears for the Deaf, a group that trains hearing assistance dogs. The County Sheriff K-9 unit and the County Search and Rescue dogs also will be on hand for demonstrations of their unique skills. Canines and their humans will be able to try out the shelter's new agility course and check out the shelter cats, dogs, puppies, and kittens available for adoption.

They say that every dog has his day. In North Idaho, that day is September 25 at the Bow Wow Pow Wow!

###

Bow Wow Pow Wow: Follow-Up Release

Here's the final follow up "thank you" Bow Wow Pow Wow press release. Again, we made sure to include the names of everyone who won anything. In the local newspaper the story ran with a lot of great photos of people having fun with their dogs.

FOR IMMEDIATE RELEASE

Contact: Susan Daffron, Animal Shelter Public Relations, at xxx-xxx-xxxx

Bow Wow Pow Wow Was a Wagging Good Time

The blustery weather didn't phase fun-loving canines or their owners on Saturday at the Animal Shelter's Bow Wow Pow Wow. The event moved inside and everyone who attended the festivities seemed to have a great time. This year, there were more dogs and more contests. A total of 108 dogs (vs. 80 last year) competed in contests ranging from Cute Miss to Most Mysterious Heritage.

People and canines filled the bleachers, enjoying demonstrations by dogs from County Search & Rescue, the County Sheriff's Office, and Dogs for the Deaf. Although most people brought their favorite canine companion, others attended without dogs just to watch the fun. Jane Smith, one of the organizers of the event, called the Bow Wow Pow Wow a "great success and a wonderful thing for the animals in this area." In fact, all the proceeds from the Bow Wow Pow Wow are already being given back to the community in the form of $10-off spay/neuter coupons.

The Animal Shelter would like to thank [big list of local companies] for their help in making this year's Bow Wow Pow Wow a reality.

We'd also like to extend big congratulations to all the contest winners!

———————————————————————————————

At the end of the press release, I also included a list of the first-, second- and third-place prizewinners in all the contests, which included

- Mr. Manners
- Miss Manners
- Best Smiling Face
- Best Tail Wagger
- Most Mysterious Heritage

- Best Begging Face
- Talent Show
- Dog/Owner Look-alike
- Handsome Hunk (lightweight)
- Cute Miss (petite)
- Handsome Hunk (heavyweight)
- Cute Miss (queen size)

Any time you can include specific names in your press release, do it. The newspaper won't always have room to print a whole list of contest winners like they did in this case, but when they do, you'll get a lot of feedback!

As an aside, I'm proud to say that at the Bow Wow Pow Wow my dog Leia won second place in the Miss Manners competition. I still have the ribbon hanging on my wall.

Publicity in Action

Case Study: Citizens for a No-Kill Philadelphia

Here's a case study that shows how Citizens for a No-Kill Philadelphia used TV along with other publicity tactics to promote their "With Love - Super Adoption Day."

Garrett R. Elwood says:

The goal of our publicity campaign was to promote our "With Love - Super Adoption Day," which is the largest adoption event in Philadelphia history, with more than 100 vendors, dozens of rescues, and fun for the whole family. The event helps promote adoption and support the great rescues and shelters that struggle every day to save lives. Our group is called Citizens for a No-Kill Philadelphia, and we wanted to show that by working together, we'll see the day when Philadelphia is a no-kill city.

The event was also used as a platform to educate Philadelphia taxpayers and pet lovers about the problems (and solutions) related to Philadelphia Animal Control, where 30,000 animals end up every year.

To get the word out, we used press releases, television appearances, heavy social media networking, radio, and print. We leveraged the PR to secure in-kind media sponsors and were able to reach a wide audience. Television was the most effective tactic we used, but it was challenging because we didn't have an advertising budget.

The first year, we had several thousand people attend and reached a very large audience. The mayor even attended and gave an award honoring a pit bull named Sarge (along with his mom) for their humane education efforts. It was the largest adoption event in Philadelphia history. We were very satisfied with how everything went, especially considering it was the event's first year. We hope to get paying sponsors this year to help offset the cost and make the event bigger and better.

Don't undervalue the service that you are providing as a nonprofit. You have to run your organization like a business. Negotiate terms, leverage the positive PR and media exposure, demonstrate return on investment, and sell your mission and organization's vision.

Citizens for a No-Kill Philadelphia: www.PhillyNoKill.org

Get Photo Opportunities

Make sure you have a camera with you as often as possible. You never know when you'll catch an adorable photo featuring one of your pets. For example, many small towns host parades for holidays like the Fourth of July. If your shelter participates in the event, enlist a volunteer to take photos of people marching the adoptable dogs in the parade.

If one of your volunteers is an amateur or pro photographer, so much the better. Many people love taking photographs, and you can take advantage of that fact by encouraging them to engage in their hobby and help homeless animals at the same time.

If your animals are at an adopt-a-thon or you put on regular "yappy hours" at local businesses, be ready for moments of extreme cuteness and snap a bunch of photos. With digital photography, it costs the same to take 10 or 1000 photos, so take a lot. If you get great shots, share them with the local newspaper. If you take pictures of people, you may need to get permission (called a "photo release"), so find out if the newspaper does that or you need to get a form. (Do a search online for photo releases and you'll find a lot of sample documents.)

After all, how many times have you seen cute photos of little kids and dogs or cats in the newspaper? Why shouldn't they be *your* adoptable dogs and cats?

Bow Wow Pow Wow: Sample Photo Press Release

Here's another sample press release from the Bow Wow Pow Wow that shows how you can take advantage of photo/artwork and turn it into a release. In this case, a local artist created the event t-shirt and we turned it into a photo opportunity, complete with a German Shepherd (who did get adopted, in fact).

FOR IMMEDIATE RELEASE

Contact: Susan Daffron, Animal Shelter Public Relations, at xxx-xxx-xxxx

Bow Wow Pow Wow T-Shirts Available Now

Artist Bonnie Shields has done it again! A limited printing of 50 Bow Wow Pow Wow t-shirts are available now for a $15 donation. The 100% cotton shirts are silk-screened with Bonnie's new Bow Wow Pow Wow artwork and are on display at the shelter.

The Animal Shelter's second annual Bow Wow Pow Wow will be held on September 25 from 11:00 am to 4:00 p.m. at the County Fairgrounds. All proceeds from the event benefit spay/ neuter cost-assistance programs at the shelter. Billed as *the* canine social event of the year, the Bow Wow Pow Wow features lots of fun contests, prizes, and demonstrations.

This year, the Bow Wow Pow Wow is sponsored by local Sandpoint veterinary clinics Animal Medical Care, Bonner Animal Hospital, North Idaho Animal Hospital, and Pend Oreille Veterinary Clinic. There will be information booths on pet care and a special visit from Ears for the Deaf, a group that trains hearing-assistance dogs. The County Sheriff K-9 unit and the County Search and Rescue dogs also will be on hand for demonstrations of their unique skills. Canines and their humans will be able to try out the shelter's new agility course and check out the shelter cats, dogs, puppies, and kittens that will be available for adoption on site at the Bow Wow Pow Wow.

PHOTO CAPTION:

Bonnie Shields models her latest t-shirt creation for the Animal Shelter's second annual Bow Wow Pow Wow along with Kit, a German Shepherd mix, who is currently available for adoption at the shelter.

Go Local

Here's something a lot of PR people don't talk about: local media is your friend. I live in a small town, and here our local paper will print almost anything.

Most local papers are like that, in fact. They are desperate for as much local news as they can get. If you have a good story and can write well, you've just made an editor or reporter's life easier, because you can do a lot of the work for them. Most newspapers are struggling with too few reporters and writers, so if you can write a good story, you are virtually guaranteed to get some ink.

The press releases you saw in the previous section, which I wrote for the Bow Wow Pow Wow, were not works of great literary art. But every single press release I wrote for that animal shelter was picked up by the local paper. I'm not kidding; *every single one* was picked up for the four years I wrote press releases for the shelter.

Most local papers are focusing on ad sales to stay alive, but they still need editorial content too. Be their go-to person for all things animal-related and you'll be able to get press any time you need it. If you partner with one of the newspaper's big advertisers on an event, even better!

It's easier to get into the publicity groove if you start small. Every local area has a small freebie newspaper. It's less intimidating to contact them than it is to deal with a huge newspaper like the Los Angeles *Times*. Once you've had some local success, jump to larger media. If you include links to articles or a list of all the mentions you've received in the media on your Web site, you can show the "big guys" you're newsworthy!

Here are a few ways you can leverage local media:

1. Write press releases and come up with a calendar Once you've worked with a local editor for a while, see if you can get a column. (I wrote a pet-care column called Pet Tails for many years and people *still* ask me about it!) Local newspapers are desperate for content; be creative and think of ways to give them some.

2. Send letters to the editor. Comment frequently on local animal-related news items.

3. Create tip sheets. These are great "filler" materials that editors love, like "Seven Ways to Keep Your Dog Safe During the Summer."

4. Keep up with local news and become the go-to source for animal-related stories.

When your local media outlets have pet questions, give them answers!

Publicity in Action

Case Study: Humane Society of West Michigan

Here's a case study that shows how the Humane Society of West Michigan took advantage of local media to help a cat named Hadley.

Marketing and Events Coordinator Nicole Cook says:

One of our most successful publicity campaigns revolved around a cat named Hadley. Hadley was a cat that was brought to us with third-degree burns over his ears, neck, back, and legs. Someone had soaked him in accelerant and then lit him on fire. The person responsible for this gruesome crime was never found, but Hadley has made an astonishing recovery and has captured the hearts of everyone who meets him.

Hadley required extensive medical treatment in order to survive. To attempt to find the person responsible and to ask people to help fund Hadley's medical bills, we created a major publicity campaign.

We used press releases and lots of local media to get the word out about Hadley. We had numerous television and radio interviews. We also created a Facebook account for Hadley (www.facebook.com/hadley.hswm), which we used to keep people informed about his progress. Hadley's Facebook account received a lot of feedback and he still has over a thousand friends today who are always curious to find out what Hadley is up to.

Although it was a challenge to keep up with the responses and donations of people who saw our publicity campaign, we received over $20,000 from all over the world for Hadley's medical expenses! The campaign was a complete success we are thrilled to report that Hadley is doing very well and has been adopted.

Humane Society of West Michigan: www.hswestmi.org

Pitch Stories to Reporters

You may have heard the term "pitch" used in reference to the media. Many people wonder how to "pitch a reporter," for example. A pitch is really just telling the media about your story without doing an official press release. You either call or e-mail a reporter with just one or two sentences about the story. You have about three seconds to get the reporter's attention, so your pitch needs to be good.

When you pitch, be sure to avoid sounding desperate. Reporters don't care if you need publicity; they care about the news. You need to frame your story around something they care about like trends or topics that relate to timely news or events. How does what you're doing relate to something larger? For example, if you've set up an adoption program specifically for seniors, you can cite some of the many studies showing that having a pet can help seniors live longer, more fulfilling lives.

Always research the media outlet before you pitch. It doesn't make any sense to pitch a story about a local event to a newspaper on the other side of the country. In much the same way, it doesn't make sense to pitch a story about your new senior adoption program to a magazine targeted to teenagers. Think about how your story relates to the paper's readers. What's in it for them? Is there a way you could redraft the pitch so it works? For example, maybe the teen magazine would be interested in a story about how teens are making a difference for the animals by starting a dog-walking program at your shelter.

Understanding a reporter's deadlines also increases your chances of success. Reporters on a deadline don't want to talk to anyone, so if you call when they are busy, you are just more likely to annoy the person and you won't get coverage. If you contact a reporter by phone, you should ask, "Is this a good time to talk?" If the person says he's on a deadline, don't ask him to call you back (he won't). Instead, ask him when might be a better time to talk.

If you plan to send a pitch or call, it helps to contact the reporter at a time of day when she won't be distracted. For example:

The deadline for TV reporters is three hours before the newscast. (It's unlikely your news counts as "breaking news" so they don't want to talk to you right before the show.)

Daily newspaper reporters file their stories between 6:00 and 7:00 p.m., so don't call after 3:00 p.m.

Reporters who write for a "Sunday" supplement often have Thursday deadlines. Don't call on deadline day.

Surf to the Web site to see what type of reporter you're dealing with and to get an idea of his or her deadline. If you are successful and get the reporter's attention, also make sure you have follow-up information you can send.

Don't forget to follow up. Being polite, yet persistent can yield big dividends. Plan to follow up by e-mail or phone about once/week.

Case Study: Outlawing Cat Declawing

Here's a case study that shows how a publicist and a veterinarian used phone pitching to capture the attention of major media and win a victory for the cats of West Hollywood.

PR professional Tom Brennan says:

The goal of our publicity campaign was to inspire a national movement that would be effective in outlawing cat declawing and finding a way to demonstrate the cruelty of the procedure.

Rather than doing a symbolic and outrageous campaign targeting lawmakers with attacks of red paint and so forth, we opted for an inspirational and positive approach. Our goal was to get declawing outlawed locally and demonstrate that this model could be replicated in other locations around the USA.

My friend Scarlet Rivera, who is well known as the violinist on the Bob Dylan classic "Hurricane," had a friend named Jennifer Conrad, a veterinarian who lived in West Hollywood. We thought that with a little push of some kind, we could convince the city council that taking a stand against declawing was a great story. Jennifer Conrad hired me at the end of 2002, and comedian Buddy Hackett's widow Shirley paid for the campaign.

The biggest foundation of the campaign was individually pitching the story on the phone to the local Los Angeles media. I had written a couple of press releases that we felt hadn't garnered enough interest. My friend Scarlet knew I could speak with personality and vivid detail to make the story compelling. She and Jennifer were banking on me to get the story through to the media. I was passionate about the cause because I had a beautiful cat named Tuesday who had changed my life and shown me the great benefits that owning a cat can bring.

Our decision to focus our pitching on print (*Los Angeles Times* and all local papers) and local news affiliates KNBC, KCBS, and KABC was key to the success of the campaign. We did a demonstration segment of Jennifer fixing a cat's paw after it had been through the horrifying process of de-clawing. Jennifer didn't invent the operation and she's not an extremist; she's just a veterinarian who was repairing the harm done by declawing.

We had to overcome a media bias against animal causes and learn how we could translate medical information into a story people could understand and then champion. Jennifer was kind enough and wise enough to open her office to news cameras so the operation could be taped and shown. When I pitched I also was able to entice even jaded news people by letting them know that if they showed the repair operation, it could help raise attention and support the referendum on the ballot in West Hollywood.

We started the campaign in December 2002. By April 2003, the Anti-Declawing Law was passed and it inspired other cities to do the same. It was a galvanizing victory for the city of West Hollywood and the People of LA. I also had Mayor James Hahn, the mayor of Los Angeles at the time, give a certificate to Jennifer Conrad in recognition of her contribution.

Tom Brennan Media: www.tombrennanpr.com

Be an Expert Source

Another way to pitch reporters is to sign up for e-mail lists of media leads. Reporters are always looking for stories and expert sources. E-mail lists are designed to connect expert sources with reporters. Here are some of the better known ones:

Help a Reporter Out (HARO), www.helpareporter.com

HARO is the wildly successful brainchild of publicist Peter Shankman. Both journalists and experts love it, partly because it's free. Journalists post queries and e-mails are sent out three times a day to a list of more than 100,000 people. Each query has an e-mail link, so you can respond to the reporter with your pitch. The main downside to HARO is the volume. If you're hoping to be used as a source, the competition is fierce. And from the journalist side, if you post a HARO query, you can expect a deluge of e-mail.

ProfNet / PRLeads, www.prleads.com

ProfNet is an expensive service that has been around for a long time, connecting reporters and sources. A somewhat less expensive option is PR Leads, which is essentially a reseller for ProfNet. For $99/month you receive queries that match the topic areas you've listed on the site. The price also includes a listing in the ProfNet expert database, which is available for journalists to search when they don't want to post a query. Because it's a paid service, the competition with other sources is not as high as it is with HARO.

Reporter Connection, www.reporterconnection.com

This service is a HARO clone from Bill and Steve Harrison, who offer expensive publicity-related products for book authors. Like HARO it's free, but it's somewhat overwhelmed by ads for the Harrison's products. Additionally, if you post a query that they think "competes" with any of their products, they won't run the query. Personally, I haven't heard of anyone who has ever gotten any publicity by using this service, but you never know.

How to Respond to Queries

When you deal with a service like Help a Reporter Out (HARO), your pitch is competing with potentially hundreds of other e-mails flooding the query poster's inbox. I've been on the receiving end of that e-mail onslaught, so here are some tips for getting your pitch noticed.

1. **Read the rules** of the service. HARO, for example, has the "Five Rules of HARO," which more or less states that you won't send off-topic pitches, you won't spam reporters, or do other slimy things. Pay attention to the rules. HARO founder Peter Shankman says he frequently bans people from HARO for violating the rules. Don't be the person who gets booted.

2. **Respond only to queries for which you are truly qualified** and follow the directions. If someone says, "Put 'Dog Story' in the subject line" or that you need to respond to a certain e-mail address, make sure you do.

3. **Be speedy**. Many people don't get a response simply because they are too slow. Remember that reporters are on a deadline. If you are a perfect fit for the story, reporters want to hear from you, but not after their

deadline. Sometimes people will set the deadline for a far-off date, but will close the query early, so don't be complacent. The reality is that the reporter is going through potentially hundreds of responses. Once he has enough, he won't consider yours. Being fast and concise matters.

4. **Don't suggest other people** as sources. It's not helpful to send an e-mail that says, "I have a friend who would be perfect." Instead, e-mail your friend and tell her to respond to the query herself. I can't tell you how many "my friend would be great" responses I get, and they are just plain annoying.

5. **Send complete contact information**. Make sure you include all possible ways to get in touch with you, including your name, business name, Web site, telephone numbers, cell phone numbers, and so forth. Many people posting queries want to check you out, so make it easy for them to find out more about you with online links. Avoid sending attachments unless a reporter explicitly asks for something.

6. **Provide answers**. If the query asks a question like "what are three ways to deal with barking dogs?" offer up some bullet points. Don't just reply with "I know the answer, call me." Remember, you always want to make the reporter's job easy. I can promise you that if you say, "e-mail me and I'll tell you," the reporter won't do it.

7. **If possible, address your response to the person by name.** Usually you'll see a name on the query, so don't say, "To whom it may concern." Use the person's name, so the response is personalized. No one likes a canned response, and rest assured reporters have no qualms about pressing the Delete key.

Case Study: Tails of The Tundra Siberian Husky Rescue

Here's a case study that shows how the Tails of the Tundra Siberian Husky Rescue used Help a Reporter Out (HARO) to get the word out about their organization.

Bob Baker works with both the Tails of the Tundra Siberian Husky Rescue and another organization called Save Our Siberians-Siberspace Rescue Fund. He says:

Although I regularly send out press releases announcing events such as our Annual Tails of the Tundra Tails on the Trails Husky Hike, my greatest successes in reaching a larger audience of potential participants and donors have come from responding to queries posted on Help A Reporter Out (www. helpareporter.com).

Recently, for example, I responded to a query from an editor of *Feathers, Fins and Fur* (www.feathersfinsandfur.com) requesting information on dog rescue groups. After several e-mail exchanges, this resulted in the publication of an article in the February issue that mentioned not only Tails of the Tundra, but another organization in which I actively participate, called Save Our Siberians-Siberspace Rescue Fund, which provides financial assistance to Siberian Husky rescue groups with dogs facing unusual or unexpected veterinary expenses. I serve not only as PR chair, but also as applications coordinator for this organization.

Every day I scan the daily HARO e-mails for other opportunities to create awareness of Siberian Husky Rescue in general and Tails of the Tundra and SOS-SRF in particular.

I also responded to a query from the author of a new book, to be published by Simon & Schuster in early 2012, titled,

The Divinity of Dogs. She was seeking inspirational stories about how dogs—especially rescue dogs—are able to relate to people in almost miraculous ways. I sent her the story of one of our foster dogs named Damona and her experience with a severely autistic child who actually responded to her in a most remarkable way. The author recently notified me that this story has been selected as a chapter in the book. It of course mentions Tails of the Tundra, too.

Tales of the Tundra: www.siberescue.com

Siberspace Rescue Fund: www.sos-srf.org

Write Articles

Tip sheets are a great way to increase the number of press releases you can put out. If you're struggling to come up with tip sheets, consider repurposing other things you've written as press releases. Often you can find a way to create a news release that talks about trends or provides advice.

For example, suppose you want to do a series of press releases on the topic of pet adoption. Here a few thoughts for identifying tips and trends:

- Are people adopting more or fewer pets because of the recession? Adopting may cost less than buying a pet from a breeder, but is pet ownership down overall? Provide the answers. Or you could write a few tips for saving money on pet expenses, such as purchasing brushes and learning how to groom your dog yourself, instead of taking him to a groomer.

- Does getting a "free" pet from the classifieds really save money? Over the years I've written a number of articles about how free puppies and kittens are not really such a great deal. When you adopt, you get a vet exam, spaying/neutering and other goodies, so the initial purchase price covers a lot. (People don't know these things, so tell them!)

- Are certain types of dog "fashionable"? What do you think of the recent "doodle" trend? Is a Labradoodle just a mutt with a fancy name? People who want these designer mutts can find dozens at your shelter!

If you have a blog, it's easy to convert your existing articles into press releases. You can use slightly reworked versions to get a second round of visibility for your organization by submitting the press releases to distribution sites. Those links bring more traffic to your Web site and more visibility for you in the search engines.

If you have a lot of content sitting around, reuse it! The trick is to rewrite the information in third person and to remove anything even remotely "sales copy-ish" from the release. Try to avoid using the word "you" as well. And remember, you want your revised text to have the relevant "who, what, where, when, why, how" as close to the beginning of the press release as possible.

Publicity in Action

Sample Press Release from an Article

Here's an example of a tips press release that was repurposed from articles. In my case, the goal was to mention my book, but there's no reason you can't mention your rescue group or animal shelter in much the same way. The idea is that you want the release to be helpful, not something that's a promotional "puff piece." Think of it as an article that's just tweaked for a different audience (i.e., the media).

Seven Ways Animal Shelters and Rescue Groups Can Raise More Money

SANDPOINT, IDAHO - For people who work to save homeless animals, it's been a rough year. Donations are down and the number of animals coming into shelters and rescue groups is up. Humane and animal rescue organizations that devise creative fundraising strategies now are more likely to hit their fundraising target next year.

Author and founder of the National Association of Pet Rescue Professionals Susan Daffron offers seven tips for how rescue groups can raise more money this year, based on her book *Funds to the Rescue: 101 Fundraising Ideas for Humane and Animal Rescue Groups* (ISBN: 978-0-9749245-9-5).

1. Craft a clear message. If people don't understand the rescue organization's mission and message, they won't donate. In some communities, humane groups struggle for donations simply because no one knows who they are, or because they are being confused with another animal-related organization. Ensure your message is clear and differentiated from others.

2. Increase outreach. Many rescue groups rely on the same outreach techniques they have used for years. In a world increasingly cluttered with marketing messages, rescue groups must explore new ways of connecting with potential donors. If you don't have an online presence, get one.

3. Embrace planning. Humane and rescue organizations that struggle financially inevitably have not crafted a fundraising plan. Create a calendar and plot out all of the organization's fundraising activities for the year, then methodically work the plan month by month.

4. Partner with other animal organizations. The amount of petty political infighting in the humane world does nothing to help the animals. Reach out to other organizations and work together on fundraising events. Multiple groups working together can generate more exposure for everyone.

5. Stay alert for new opportunities to connect. The more ways people can engage with a rescue organization, the more fundraising opportunities can result.

6. Set goals. Each fundraising activity should have written financial goals and objectives. Understanding the "why" and "how much" of the activity helps keeps everyone on track.

7. Work with others in the community. Many of the ideas in *Funds to the Rescue* are partnerships between a local business and a humane group. The type of business is almost irrelevant. Businesses from hair salons to car dealers have been recruited to raise money for animals.

The author of *Funds to the Rescue*, Susan Daffron, says, "The money is out there, but people need to get creative in their fundraising in order to attract attention."

About Funds to the Rescue

Funds to the Rescue: 101 Fundraising Ideas for Humane and Animal Rescue Groups is $19.95 and available through major online booksellers and at www.FundstotheRescue.com. At the book Web site, visitors can receive a free special report called "Paws-i-tively Easy Fundraising Ideas: Five Simple and Fun Fundraisers You Can Put Together Quickly." For information on other products, visit the publisher's Web site at www. logicalexpressions.com.

About Susan Daffron

Susan Daffron is founder of the National Association of Pet Rescue Professionals (www.naprp.com), a membership association made up of people who are working for animal shelters, humane societies or rescue groups. Daffron is also the author of eleven books, including two books on caring for adopted pets. She is a former veterinary assistant, animal shelter volunteer, employee, and nonprofit board member. She also owns a publishing and software company called Logical Expressions, Inc.

About Logical Expressions, Inc.

Logical Expressions is a book- and software-publishing company based in Sandpoint, Idaho, that is owned by Susan Daffron and James Byrd. The company offers books, software, tools, and services that help businesses with print and online publishing projects. In addition to publishing its own series of books, Logical Expressions offers book production services. They help guide people through the steps to become a successful independent book publisher.

###

Be creative with this concept! You can take an article and tie the content to a trend, the season, or a series of tips. Over the years, I tied a press release about an online conference to travel trends, one about pet care tips to President Obama's puppy, and a seasonal release about dealing with huge quantities of summer zucchini.

Publicity in Action

Case Study: Bow Wow Buddies Foundation

Here's a case study that shows how a nonprofit foundation called Bow Wow Buddies used a series of press releases to raise awareness.

PR professional Jocelyn Kahn says:

The goal of our publicity campaign was not only to publicize the On Our Way Home Project's goals and Camp Bow Wow's nonprofit organization, the Bow Wow Buddies Foundation, but to raise awareness for the conditions in many shelters across the country, ultimately resulting in additional donations to the project (to fund the $50K grant).

We distributed press releases at each stage during the project (the call for entries, when entries closed, and the winner announcement). We also pitched local and national media about shelter conditions and took advantage of our strong social media presence on Facebook and Twitter. By pitching and sending press releases to targeted media, we successfully got the word out about the foundation.

The only issue we had was that we didn't have applicants from every state in the US, so it was difficult to secure media coverage in areas without applicants, even though we were trying to make it a national initiative. It also was difficult to show the importance of the project because it was the inaugural year and we didn't have any case studies to show success. Next time we will use case studies from the success in our first year to show the importance of the project.

Thanks to the campaign, donations increased, traffic to the Camp Bow Wow Web site increased, and we received more recognition for both Camp Bow Wow and its nonprofit Foundation. We raised awareness for the plight of shelter dogs and the importance of socialization and adoption.

Camp Bow Wow: www.campbowwow.com

5W PR: www.5wpr.com

Get on the Radio

The radio is another great source of free publicity. Maybe you think no one listens to the radio anymore, but that's not true. If you've ever spent time commuting to work or sat in a traffic jam, you know that radio can feel like your best friend during a boring or aggravating drive. Many people around you on the freeway are listening to talk radio, sometimes for hours every day.

Radio can work particularly well in rural areas where there aren't a lot of radio stations. Many of those local stations have a community events calendar and a local news program on which your event can be mentioned. Often you can just send an e-mail or a fax to get a mention. Of course, you also can pitch your story to a radio producer and see if you can get an interview. Some local stations also have commentators or community-issues shows that have a constant need for guests.

Here in our little town in Idaho, for many years an animal shelter board member did a little blurb every week about one of the animals available for adoption. Because she has a fabulous British accent, her voice was distinctive. She told me once that people at the grocery store would ask her if she was the "dog lady" on the radio. Of course, she admitted she was and encouraged people to adopt their next pet from the shelter.

Radio PSAs

Another simple way to get on the radio is to take advantage of the fact that radio stations have to give a certain amount of airtime to nonprofits in the form of Public Service Announcements or PSAs. Broadcast media outlets are required by the Federal Communications Commission (FCC) to serve "in the public interest" and many radio and television stations use PSAs as one method of meeting the requirement. Basically, a PSA is an advertisement that is intended to raise awareness of or educate the public about an issue.

You can do a PSA in two ways. You can send the station either ready-to-use audio or a script that the announcer can read live. If you remember phrases like "This is your brain on drugs" or "Friends don't let friends drive drunk," you recognize an effective slogan that was used in a PSA campaign from the Ad Council.

The airtime for PSAs is donated, but you may incur some cost if you opt to do your own production. You're competing with other nonprofits for that coveted airtime, so make sure you come up with a clear message and a call to action. PSAs are most effective when they encourage someone to do (or not do) something like avoiding drugs or drunk driving. For example, a rescue group could do a campaign that encourages adoption or spaying/neutering pets.

To find out more about PSAs, you should contact your local broadcast media outlet(s). If it's a small station, ask to talk to the station manager or the person in charge of selecting PSAs. See what they look for in PSAs, if there is a particular audio format they need, and how long the PSA should be. Then go forth and create a pithy and compelling message, and get it out there!

Get Interviewed on Radio Shows

Another tried-and-true method of getting publicity is getting yourself booked on a radio show. The authors of *Chicken Soup for the Soul* have said that they did literally hundreds of telephone interviews with radio stations across the country to help sell their books. You can take the same approach, even if it's on a somewhat smaller scale. If you adopt animals locally, you should focus on your local area, but if you live in a metropolitan area like Los Angeles, there could be literally hundreds of radio shows that would love to book you as a guest.

Although you can buy lists of radio stations, it's more cost-effective to compile your own. This site has a link to every radio station:

http://radio-locator.com/

You enter a zip code and it will return the call sign, frequency, signal, city, school, and format. If you click the little "i" icon, you will get information such as the owner's name, street address, and phone number. The call sign is also a the link to the radio station's Web site, if they have one, so you will be able to get more specific contact information before you make your pitch.

Get on TV

It may seem far-fetched to get your critters on TV, but it's not as hard as you might think. You have a number of ways to use the power of television to help spread the word about your adoptable animals. Here are three possible ways you might be able to get your fifteen minutes of fame on TV.

1. Cable access TV
2. TV talk shows
3. News programs.

Cable Access TV

By law, cable TV companies are required to offer "public access" channels to their lineup. These public or cable access TV stations are set aside by cable companies for public, educational, or governmental (PEG) use. Often cable access stations are run by a nonprofit organization or a local government.

For example, Fitchburg Access Television (FATV) is a 501(c)(3) organization that operates the PEG access channels on the cable television system in Fitchburg, Massachusetts. According to their Web site fatv.org, viewers can find FATV on Comcast Cable in Fitchburg on channels 8 (public), 9 (educational), and 10 (government) and via Verizon and Fitchburg State

College. FATV is just one of about 2,000 cable access providers throughout the country.

As a nonprofit, it can be remarkably easy to get airtime on these stations. In fact, when I visited the FATV Web site, it was advertising "PSA Day," which offered local nonprofits a free opportunity to promote their services by taping a thirty-second and sixty-second Public Service Announcement (PSA).

Many cable access channels also offer classes and workshops so you can learn how to use the equipment and produce your own shows. For example, Marblehead Cable Access (marbleheadtv.org) offers a five-week class in video production. The classes are designed to teach studio production techniques using studio equipment, and location production techniques using the station's portable equipment. Once students finish the class, they are certified to produce shows for the channel or help other producers.

The first step is to contact your local public access TV station(s) and learn more about their programming. You can find a lot of information online or simply contact your cable company. See if the cable access station offers courses on video production; many now offer information about Internet TV as well.

TV Talk Shows

Once you have some TV experience under your belt, whether through your own show or from being interviewed locally, you can experiment with pitching the big-time TV talk show folks, asking to be a guest. Bear in mind you have to have a huge story and the competition is fierce.

This page has links to many of the major talk shows:

http://www.interbridge.com/lineups.html

If you actually get a producer's attention, when that person calls you, you need to be aware that it's not just a friendly conversation. The caller is "testing" to see if you will be a good guest. Think of it as an interview and try to be as creative and helpful as possible. Also, you may have to be available on a moment's notice if the big interview day comes suddenly.

Sometimes slots open up and you have to rush to make the show, or you could get "bumped" and have to reschedule. Your job is to be the great guest who doesn't get cranky, even when you have to cater to big scheduling changes and snafus. The resulting publicity is worth some inconvenience.

Publicity in Action

Case Study: D Cups Saving Tea Cups

Here's a case study that shows how a group called D Cups Saving Tea Cups got national attention by getting on a TV show.

Founder Kim Sill says:

The D Cups are a group of dedicated women working to save animals through fundraisers, media, and humane pet shops. I wanted to reach a national audience, so I videotaped a puppy mill dog that I rescued and sent the tape to the producers of "The Dog Whisperer." The video resulted in a one hour special about puppy mills, where I took Cesar Milan to a puppy mill.

I used a variety of publicity tactics, including press releases, and I was very specific in who I sent them to. I made sure that I e-mailed the producer who would make decisions about the upcoming stories. When I was deciding whom to send newspaper story ideas to, I went through past articles written about animals and targeted those writers.

I was contacted after being on the local news and that exposure brought the most donations and led to other media opportunities. During the campaign, it was important to think ahead and to have a "twist."

Whenever I was pitching a story, I needed to put a lot of thought into the pitch. I tried to use the names of celebrities who are popular, like Lady Gaga. (I named a *lot* of dogs Lady Gaga last year!) The campaign resulted in a lot of adoptions to high-profile celebrities and media attention, which increased my donor base.

It has been an incredible journey. My passion for saving animals led me to become a force and a voice for them

D Cups Saving Teacups: www.dcupssavingteacups.com

Get Quoted
or Featured in
Magazines

Being quoted or featured in a magazine is a great publicity coup. Targeting animal-related publications is a good place to start. This approach makes sense, because these publications are read by the people who are most likely to be interested in what you do. Their readership cares about animals, so their writers are looking for story ideas. Many larger communities have a freebie animal-related publication, so if you're just starting out, writing for a free publication can be a great way to practice your article writing and get a few clips.

If you rescue a particular type of animal, like ferrets, you'll want to target publications like *Ferrets Magazine* first. However, with that said, don't stop at just one idea; look at your subject from more than one angle. For example, you could suggest a profile of your ferret rescue for your local business magazine. Or pitch a "how to take care of your child's new ferret" article for a woman's magazine. Or "how to introduce your new ferret to the cat" for a cat-related magazine.

Here are a few pet publications to get you started:

- Tails Pet Media Group Inc. - www.tailsinc.com. Outlet for news pertaining to pets and their appearances in media.

- Total Pet Publishing - www.totalpetpublishing.com. This company owns several pet-related Web sites, directories, and services. Most are dog-related, but they also have sites relating to cats and rabbits.

- Pet Planet Magazine - www.petplanetmagazine.com. "The Pet Planet Magazine® is a fun and informative pet-resource magazine with a strong focus on our pet community and pet rescue!"

- Pet Age - www.petage.com. A popular business-to-business magazine for workers in the pet retail trade.

- Housepet - www.housepetmagazine.com. An online magazine catering to the health and longevity of pets.

- Pet News Now - www.petnewsnow.net. A leading resource for pet news and information. Membership is free.

- Modern Dog - www.moderndogmagazine.com. "The lifestyle magazine for modern dogs and their companions."

- Animal People Newspaper - www.animalpeoplenews.org. "The leading independent publication covering animals and animal protection efforts worldwide..."

- The Bark - www.thebark.com "A magazine about life with dogs - written for readers who appreciate its motto dog is my co-pilot. Topics explore behavior & health, recreation & travel, culture & community; art & literature - plus great cartoons."

- Cat Fancy - www.catchannel.com/magazines/catfancy/ Every month's issue features a different breed of cat, as well as lifestyle news for cat lovers. It has won several awards for editorial content.

- Dog Fancy - www.dogchannel.com/dfdc_portal.aspx. "Dog Fancy is a monthly magazine dedicated to dogs, owners of dogs, and breeders of dogs. It was founded in 1970 and is described by its publishing company BowTie Inc. as the world's most widely read dog magazine."

- Dog's Life - www.dogslifemagazine.com A heartfelt magazine dedicated to enriching the lives of canine companions.
- Bird Talk - www.birdchannel.com/bird-magazines/bird-talk/ A magazine for the parrot and pet-bird lover.
- Ferrets Magazine - www.smallanimalchannel.com/ferrets-magazine/ For owners and fanciers of ferrets. Also contains links to other small-pet resources, such as hamsters, chinchillas, sugar gliders and gerbils.
- Pet Enthusiast - pe-magazineblog.com. News and information for pet lovers.

This list is just the tip of a very large iceberg. Many more pet publications exist. Do some online searches and visit your local library for more ideas.

Publicity in Action

Case Study: Linens for Animals

Here's a case study that shows how Linens for Animals targeted magazines to raise awareness about their programs and sanctuary.

Lori Birdsong says:

My overall goal for publicity is always two-fold: first, to distribute linens in every U.S. community for animals in need. Second, to raise awareness for adoptions and funding for the Linens for Animals No Kill Dog & Cat Shelter/Sanctuary.

A large portion of the attention Linens for Animals received was through self-promotion and community relations. Every time I came across an animal-related magazine, I would write to the editor, tell them about our unique organization and encourage them to write an article about us. Fortunately, many of those editors went to our Web site and agreed! For the grand opening of our Shelter/Sanctuary in June 2010, we tried something else and hired HCK2 Partners in Addison to distribute a regional press release. It created a good deal of local interest from regional news outlets, including the Collin County Business Press and Dallas Morning News.

When you have a cause as important as this, the people you work with are going to get involved. One of our linen distribution centers in Houston told a journalist who writes for *Dog Fancy* magazine about us. The journalist contacted me, and we landed a two-page article in their 40th anniversary edition. It generated calls from eight states to find out how we do what we do, so they could implement Linens for Animals in their own community. In addition, several radio stations from various states have contacted me to talk about our linens program.

Finally, community relations has been an area for awareness for us. In 2009 we accepted two Labs from a soldier who had 48 hours to deploy to Iraq. After arriving, he found out that he had cancer and was sent home. I reached out to my friend at the Houston Chronicle, who wrote about him and told about how we stepped in and raised more than $20,000 for the young man. This article created great awareness in Houston, as well as a story on TV.

I think each tactic was effective in its own way, based on our many needs. Some, such as the *Dog Fancy* article, helped call attention to the "linen" side of our mission. Social media increased awareness on the "animal shelter" side. Various stories have been key in creating awareness about Linens for Animals. In addition, rolling up my sleeves and looking for reporters to talk about us has been a lifeline for our cause and these animals. It's amazing what a little proactive searching can do!

Our biggest challenge was, and continues to be, the fact that the "linen" side is unique, and unfortunately can overshadow our shelter/sanctuary work. Although it seems there is a "better story" to tell on the "linen" side, there is an important story to share regarding our shelter and sanctuary. Getting the same amount of coverage for the shelter and sanctuary as we do for linen distribution proves to be a continuous challenge. We have no grants or sponsors to help us with operations. Being a sanctuary does not allow us the ability to have a tremendous intake and outflow. It's getting others to care about what happens after the rescue, or during rehabilitation, that is challenging, but certainly as important.

The results of our efforts are immediate. Following an article, I'll get a flood of phone calls from all over the United States asking about Linens for Animals. Facebook has really helped spread the word about our adoption days, and we are seeing an increase in adoptions because of that. All the local media attention helped to connect us with the Collin County Juvenile Probation Department, and we have created a unique partnership with them for the young people who need community service hours. We have many great kids helping us at the shelter/sanctuary and at all of our adoption days. They are helping the animals, and according to many parents' comments, the animals are helping the kids make smarter life choices.

I learn as I go, figure out what works and what doesn't, and continue to add new tools to my toolbox. For example, I had a meeting with a young man who has to serve 160 community service hours. He just happens to be a marketing guru who is going to build us a brand-new Web site, as well as "fluff up" our social media presence. Wow, what a gift!

Linens for Animals: www.LinensforAnimals.org.

Get Social

When you stop and think about it, a lot of online publicity and marketing is like high school. Little cliques and sub-niches develop in every nook and cranny of the Internet. If you ever saw the movie "Ferris Bueller's Day Off," you know Ferris was popular because (to quote Grace, the school secretary) "The sportos and motor heads, geeks, sluts, bloods, wastoids, dweebies, dickheads...they all adore him. They think he's a righteous dude."

In much the same way, for your organization's Web site and promotional efforts to get any traction online, you need to hang out where the "popular kids" are. These days that means if you want to spread the word about pretty much anything, it's important to have a presence on social media sites like Facebook and Twitter.

However, with that said, you may find smaller social sites are worthwhile to participate in as well. For example, if you're involved in rabbit rescue, you can probably find a lot of forums or social networking sites that are specific to people who love rabbits.

Facebook is currently the largest of the social networking sites. With hundreds of millions of users and growing, it is a prime way to establish connections with people who share your interests. Because people prefer to adopt pets from and donate to organizations they feel connected to, the more virtual friends you can make through social media sites, the more opportunities you will have for sharing your message.

To get started on any of these sites is simple:

1. Set up an account.

2. Follow the steps to set up your profile. Be sure to include information about your organization and your Web site or blog. If you have any video or audio files, you often can upload those, too.

3. Start making friends. You usually can upload your e-mail address book and find other people you know who already are on the networking site.

4. Put a link to your various social networking site profiles on your book site and other Web sites you own.

5. Send messages to friends or post to the "wall" in Facebook.

6. Post questions or answers to questions in your own or other groups.

Different social media sites appeal to different people. Some people like the "chatty" aspect of Twitter and other people like the fact that you can "friend" almost anybody in Facebook and post pictures, so it's more visual. Although networking online can definitely help your organization, it's easy to spend a lot of time on social media sites, so don't let it turn into a giant distraction or time sink.

Interact on Facebook

Facebook is used by literally hundreds of thousands of users every day, so it makes sense to have a presence there. However, Facebook has a habit of changing how it works constantly, which is the source of confusion for a lot of people. Fortunately, most of the big things remain the same, so here is an overview of the major elements of Facebook and how and when you should use them.

A *profile* is designed to represent an individual human being. According to the terms of service, a business cannot have a personal profile, so don't set one up for your rescue or humane group. A profile has to represent a real live person, or Facebook will shut it down. You don't want to put in a bunch of work and make a lot of connections, only to have it taken away. However, if your volunteers, board members, supporters, or other people are on Facebook, encourage them to share your message through their own personal profile. With a profile, other people can "friend" you and connect with you.

A *page* is basically a profile that can be used by a business. Pages can be set up for businesses, political or charitable organizations, celebrities, bands, personalities, and more. They mostly look and act like a regular profile, but they have more customization options and features. Posts from pages appear in a person's regular news feed, so it can be difficult to differentiate between posts from individual profiles and those from pages. In Facebook-speak, people don't "friend" a page, they "like" it. So if you create a page for your organization, you want to get lots of people to like it.

A *group* is designed to let people communicate with each other about a given topic. You can set up a group so it is public (open to everyone), closed (open only to people you invite), or hidden. Pages can't join groups; only profile accounts can become group members. Although groups work somewhat like pages, you can notify members of the group of new discussions, have chats, and create documents.

An *event* is a special page that can be set up by a profile or a page owner and is designed to provide information about an activity. If you're doing a dog-walk fundraiser, for example, you can create an event page that provides information and answers people's questions. You can invite and communicate with people about the event via e-mail and upload videos, files, and images.

Before you get too deep into Facebook, you should spend some time in the online help:

www.facebook.com/help/

In particular, you should spend some time perusing the security settings, so you will have an understanding of who is (and is not) seeing what you do in Facebook.

Publicity in Action

Case Study: Animal House Shelter, Inc.

Here's a case study that explains how the Animal House Shelter in Huntley, Illinois, used Facebook and other social media sites to open the lines of communication with people in their community.

Social media/marketing volunteer Alexis Williams says:

We wanted to use social networking to create awareness for the shelter and the animals that need homes. It has also become an effective way to announce events and news and distribute information quickly. We have seen a great sense of engagement within our presence in social networks. Our fans re-tweet our tweets and comment on our Facebook posts quite often.

In addition to using our existing Web site (www. animalhouseshelter.com), we created a Facebook page, a YouTube account, and a Twitter account (@HuntleyAHS), and used these different media to post information. Although we often don't post the same thing on each site, the different media also work together. For instance, when we post about animals available for adoption, we include a link to the animal's page on our Web site to direct the person to see more information about the animal.

Of the three social networks, Facebook has been the most effective in terms of creating engagement with our fans. Our fans leave posts telling us how things are going with animals they have adopted. They also comment on pictures, include great comments about the animals, and show enthusiasm when we post who has been adopted.

We have a great group of volunteers who help monitor and post to the social networks. Using a team has helped tremendously and kept the maintenance from being overwhelming for just one person. We are still trying to increase the number of fans and followers in all channels and incorporate links to our social networks in our e-mails and Web sites in order to gain a larger following.

The biggest success we have seen is that we have opened the line of communication between our supporters and the shelter. Instead of the one-sided communication that we previously had, the communication between the shelter and supporters now flows both ways. We receive lots of supportive comments and words of encouragement and have found Facebook to be a great place to post our events, news, and requests for assistance.

On Twitter, we have met many other great animal rescue groups that are doing the same work we are. We help each other by re-tweeting each other's tweets. Pet product companies have offered donations simply because of our presence on Twitter; we have received donations of collars and dog skin care products.

Animal House Shelter: www.animalhouseshelter.com

Set up a Facebook Page

Now that you understand the difference between a Facebook profile and a Facebook page, you probably are thinking that your organization needs a page. Setting one up is easier than you might think and it's a great way to connect with other organizations and supporters who might not find out about your organization any other way.

Facebook is actually one of the most visited sites on the Internet, and many users spend literally hours on the site. If you have video content, podcasts, interviews, or documents, you can put them on your Facebook page for free. If you integrate Facebook with other social media tools like Twitter, YouTube, Flickr, and your Web site or blog, you can expand your network and update your community with your news and information.

After you have a Facebook profile, you can create a page. The person who sets up the page is the "admin" of the page. You can add and remove admins; for security reasons, you should have more than one. Nonprofit organizations often have a revolving door of volunteers and you don't want to end up in a situation where your only Facebook page admin is no longer available.

To set up a page, you go here:

https://www.facebook.com/pages/create.php

Because Facebook changes things so often, you should refer to the site itself for more specific information about setting up your page. These reference pages are a good place to start. If you click to the Wall tab, you'll find lots of links to other helpful resources as well:

www.facebook.com/facebookpages

www.facebook.com/nonprofits

www.facebook.com/influencers

www.facebook.com/help

Facebook, and social media in general, is all about connecting with other people personally. Use your page to engage people in conversation. Ask questions and reply to comments. If people post interesting things on your wall, give them feedback. Your page also gives you the opportunity to hear what could be improved in your organization.

Once you have a page with twenty-five "likes," you can get a "vanity" URL, which is a Web address that's shorter and easier to remember. For example, my page for the National Association of Pet Rescue Professionals is www.facebook.com/naprp

After you have your vanity URL, include it in your online and offline communication to encourage people to find and "like" your organization on Facebook. Many widgets exist so you can include "like" buttons on your blog or Web site. If you really want to expand your community, you also can run Facebook ads to drive more people to your page. This page has more information on advertising:

www.facebook.com/adsmarketing/

Case Study: Austin Pets Alive

Here's a case study that shows how an animal rescue group called Austin Pets Alive (APA) got the word out about their No Kill Plan.

PR Manager Sarah Weinstein says:

Our overall goal was to make Austin, Texas a no-kill city. There are many facets to that, but the main ones we as an organization focused on were increasing adoptions and decreasing owner surrenders to the shelter. Other groups focus on spay/neuter, so we decided to put our efforts into helping the pets that have already been born and are at-risk of being killed in our city shelter.

We believe that approximately 75,000 new pets are acquired in Austin/Travis County every year, while only 22,000 are going through our city shelter. Based on these numbers and the numbers from Reno, Nevada, which is no-kill but has an even higher intake ratio compared to Austin, we don't believe that Austin has an overpopulation problem, but rather a problem of not enough people adopting from our city shelter or local rescue groups. (Reno's population is about 400,000 and their animal intake is 15,000, compared to Austin's 1,000,000 population with 22,000 intake.)

We want to show people how great rescue pets are and to make adopting a really fun, rewarding experience. We are changing the culture so that people want to adopt and be part of this no-kill movement. Our communications are always positive. You're never going to hear APA complaining about the irresponsible public. There are about 10,000 people who take pets into our city shelter every year, yet there are 600,000 homes with pets in Austin/Travis County. Instead of negative messaging directed at the 10,000 problem homes, we focus on the other 590,000 pet-lovers who might want to help.

As far as getting the word out, Facebook is huge for us. On Facebook, we have passionate fans and they love to help us spread the message around. With that said, we still think press releases are important for reaching people who aren't regularly in touch with us. We also get a pretty good response from TV stations and their coverage. We don't have a budget at all for advertising/marketing, so we don't run ads on TV, the radio, or in newspapers. We have about twelve adoption sites around the city, which have also been instrumental in getting people's attention, increasing adoptions, and getting people to think of APA! when they're looking to adopt a pet. We also use Twitter, which is very effective, although probably not as effective as Facebook.

A powerful message for us is that all of the pets we take in were once on the euthanasia list at the shelter and would have been killed in twelve hours had we not pulled them out. Many are highly desirable pets. Unfortunately, that has not made the city shelter look good. As hard as we work at providing positive messages about the city shelter, which is our partner, we are accused of bashing them. We have to work hard to keep our volunteers and supporters calm when something inflammatory comes out from someone at the city shelter or the media, so that our relations with them remain civil and supportive.

In addition, the Austin rescue community is not united. There are some who think we must be doing something irresponsible to have adoption numbers as high as ours, even though our adoption standards and adopter support are much higher than at our city shelter. We believe that we could accomplish much more together as a united community of animal rescuers, but that has not been possible. Again, we have to work hard to ensure that our volunteers and supporters remain above the fighting, by constantly staying positive and focusing on the successes and work to be done, not worrying about a recent rumor that someone has started.

The general public has been incredibly supportive of our work. In fact, Austin reached no-kill in February 2011 with 92% of the dogs and cats left alive! We have saved the lives of over 7,000 animals since the start of our adoption program in 2008 and have successfully advocated to city council to put programs in place at the city shelter to help save even more. Our volunteers give 2,000 hours per week, and we're now one of the first places people look to when adopting a pet in Austin. We also grew our budget from almost nothing in 2008 to one million dollars in our second year.

Austin Pets Alive: www.austinpetsalive.org

Tweet Your
Message

Twitter is another social media site you can use to get the word out. Most people, when taking their first look at Twitter, think it's weird at best, or utterly stupid at worst. It's true that Twitter can seem like it's doing nothing but fostering the worst type of insipid water-cooler chat among people who have nothing better to do.

However, over time many nonprofits and businesses have proven that participating in Twitter can lead to great new connections and opportunities, so don't write it off, even if you're initially somewhat confused by it. Twitter has a lot of potential for "friend-raising," marketing, and even adoptions. Because Twitter is all about immediacy, if you have an animal with a problem, the word can spread virally among people who are willing to help. It can be remarkable to witness and it really does happen all the time.

Twitter can be used to:

- Drive more traffic to your Web site.
- Reach out to contacts in the rescue/humane world that would be difficult or impossible to connect with in any other way.

- Get answers to questions quickly.

- Alert you to breaking news and industry trends (which can help in writing your press releases).

- Share information with other people.

When you get set up on Twitter, choose a name that's short and easy to remember. Start following people and lurk for a while so you can get comfortable with the Twitter culture. Then start posting a few updates. (Yes, it takes some practice thinking of intelligent things you can contribute in just 140 characters.)

Here are a few other tips:

- **Learn the lingo**. For example, RT means "retweet" and it's a way to share things other people have posted with your followers. If someone retweets something you've posted, be polite and say thank you.

- **Be professional.** Remember that you are representing your organization. Do not tweet that you are sitting in your underwear eating a Twinkie (even if you are). Yes, there is such a thing as too much information (TMI)!

- **Create a complete profile**. Use your organization's logo or a good photo. Don't leave the default picture or people will think you're a spammer. Include an intelligent, concise description of who you are and what you do.

- **Don't overdo it**. Some people tweet so much that you have to wonder if they have a life. Never shutting up is annoying and can make people wonder if you're some type of psycho or spammer.

- **Don't over-promote.** Along the same lines, don't make every tweet an advertisement or a plea for donations. Twitter is about sharing information, so if you find articles you think are helpful, share them. It doesn't always have to be just about you.

Tweet on!

Publicity in Action

Case Study: Beagle Freedom Project

Here's a case study that shows how Animal Rescue, Media & Education (ARME) and their publicists used a combination of social networking and PR to promote the Beagle Freedom Project

Kezia Jauron from Evolotus PR says:

The Beagle Freedom Project is a mission of Animal Rescue, Media & Education (ARME), founded by Shannon Keith. Working with Evolotus PR, a public relations agency owned by Kezia Jauron and Gary Smith, they used publicity to help rescue beagles from animal testing laboratories and give them a chance at life in a loving home. The campaign had the following goals:

- Raise funds to rescue, rehabilitate, and re-home dogs used in animal testing laboratories when they are no longer wanted for research purposes.

- Encourage laboratory personnel to release healthy, adoptable animals to ARME instead of destroying them.

- Inform the public that dogs are used to test personal care and health products, and encourage consumers to purchase alternative products that are not tested on animals.

We used a combination of PR and social networking (Facebook and Twitter). Media coverage and social networking work together. Whenever you have editorial coverage, you should share it on Facebook and Twitter. Doing both has much more impact than just one tactic alone.

Like most animal rescue campaigns, ours had built-in mascots/ambassadors: Freedom and Bigsby, two beagles from the organization's first rescue. Shannon had the foresight to shoot video of sweet Freedom and Bigsby being released from their cages and experiencing fresh air, sunshine, and grass for the first time. These first visuals of Freedom and Bigsby allowed members of the media and the public to connect instantly to these dogs and imagine the trauma they had endured.

We wrote a brief pitch for media, and included links to this heart-punching video. We actually didn't write a formal press release. Believing that pet lovers would be most likely to donate to our cause, our editorial pitches went primarily to journalists covering pet/animal topics and some general news. We reached out to national news, network news, local news stations throughout California, newspapers, and Web sites, including popular pet and dog-related blogs. We included journalists who had been open to animal rights topics in the past.

We also created Web site text for the campaign, which introduced people to the use of beagles in animal testing. To do this sensitively, it was written as helpful information for potential adopters, instead of stating directly that purchasing products that are tested on animals causes the testing. This was very effective, and our text was used verbatim, or nearly so, in several media placements. Animal activists are often accused of being sensationalistic or overly shocking, so we were careful to present facts that could be verified on third-party Web sites if necessary (such as Purina's LabDiet site, which provides information on the care and feeding of laboratory dogs). We included links to lists of cruelty-free products and companies that still test on animals to make it convenient for site visitors to research the issue.

Having a great video told our story to editorial contacts in a way that mere words couldn't. Every nonprofit wants to educate, but nobody particularly likes being schooled, journalists especially. We were fortunate that Beagle Freedom Project gave us the opportunity to tell an emotional, positive story that happened to be educational. This path caused people to open their hearts as well as their minds and wallets.

Animal research is a sensitive and emotionally charged subject, and we needed to approach the campaign respectfully. Research labs want to avoid any interaction with animal rights groups, so there was a risk of alienating the very people whose participation we needed: researchers in the position of deciding whether animals live or die. The name of the lab that released the first beagles was kept confidential. The unintended consequence was that this allowed us to broaden our editorial reach. Had we announced what lab we worked with, we would have more limited in our geographic market.

In six weeks of actively promoting the campaign, we raised more than $7,000 through "crowd-sourced" small, individual donations. We also received e-mails and messages from about 1,200 people who were moved to contact us and we are now close to 5,000 members on the Facebook cause page. Dozens of people in Los Angeles alone offered to adopt or foster the beagles.

We received editorial coverage in more than forty outlets in six weeks, including major city newspapers in Los Angeles, San Francisco, and Seattle; popular pet sites and blogs; TV news in San Diego, and Los Angeles; and nationally on CNN Headline News. One blog alone was shared more than 1,200 times on Facebook. We also saw nice "bumps" from coverage on political pundit (and beagle lover) Andrew Sullivan's blog, and a re-tweet by actress Alyssa Milano. CNN will be tagging along on our next rescue. In fact, in hindsight, we should have called CNN first! They were less interested in reporting on the story after it happened, and want to be included in the next rescue so they can capture the story from beginning to end.

There were more than 35,000 views of the rescue videos on YouTube, with 25,000+ resulting from PR/media hits. We know this because there were two similar videos on two different YouTube channels. We used one video solely for PR/media, so we were able to see exactly how many views resulted from our PR efforts.

Fifteen university-affiliated research labs using beagles in experiments have said they are willing to work with ARME in the future and retire adoptable dogs instead of euthanizing them.

As a result of media exposure, institutional support has come in the form of free food from V-Dog, a percentage of sales at Toesox.com, the use of a private room at the House of Blues on the Sunset Strip for a fundraiser, and a yoga studio fundraiser. Chicago-based Mark Rizzo Design, which creates the graphics on the Oprah Winfrey show, donated a logo. New York's Mobile Matters donated their services to create a text-based campaign so people could pledge by texting "beagle" to 22122. Students at elementary and middle schools have held supplies drives and collected boxes of toys, treats, bowls, collars, and leashes.

We monitored the comments and responses to stories online fairly closely. Hundreds of people mentioned they had no idea dogs are used in animal research. Better yet, they reported they were researching the products they use and throwing away their makeup. Many thoughtful conversations about animal testing occurred. Even people who approve of animal testing supported our campaign because they agree that animals should be released into homes instead of killed when they are no longer wanted.

Freedom and Bigsby were adopted quickly, and despite their years of living in cages, their personalities have begun to emerge. Freedom is "Action Jackson," while Bigsby is rather a couch potato. Freedom enjoys going on long hikes, chewing on sticks, and running in circles, whereas Bigsby appreciates soft beds, soft toys, and soft laps.

Beagle Freedom Project: www.beaglefreedomproject.org

Create Videos (YouTube and Beyond)

People love cute animals. Photos are great, but videos of your critters live and in living color can be even better. At the risk of sounding crass, a video can act like a subtle advertisement for your animals. If Fluffy does something completely and totally adorable, show it off. She'll end up "selling" people through sheer cuteness.

Even if you don't have a video camera, you can use still photos, add some transitions and a sound track, and turn it into a video. You can also incorporate Flash animation or even slides. You're limited only by your creativity.

Once you have a video, you can put it on video sites like YouTube, your own site, social networking sites, and other video-sharing sites. Although you can pay people to shoot video for you, if you don't have the budget, you can do it yourself.

Creating a video doesn't have to be particularly complicated or expensive. I've pointed out many times that I'm the only person I know who created a bunch of videos before ever getting a video camera or video software!

To assemble their videos, many people use free tools like Microsoft Movie Maker, which comes with Windows. In my case, for one of my videos I used still images and put them together using a tool called Camtasia. The bottom line is that you can create a video many different ways, so do a little research online, look at the tools you already have, and spend a little time surfing YouTube first for inspiration.

When it comes to creating your own movies, do be sure to respect copyright. If you use images, make very sure they are completely royalty-free. The same goes for music. For one of my videos I used royalty-free music from a musician's online site. Even though the audio clip I used was free, I also put a credit line and his Web site address in the closing credits of the video.

Obviously, you want to upload your video to YouTube, but a number of other video-sharing sites exist as well, such as Yahoo Video, AOL Video, and DailyMotion.com. You also can upload your videos to social media sites like Facebook. Other sites that are mostly known for photos (Flickr and Photobucket) and audio (iTunes) also let you post videos.

The key to video is to make it interesting. If you have a fun video, people may pass the link on to their friends. Ideally, it goes viral and sends a lot of people to your blog or Web site.

Publicity in Action

Case Study: Animal Rescue League of Boston

Here's a case study that shows how a volunteer for the Animal Rescue League of Boston used a video to raise money for emergency medical expenses for a severely injured dog named Turtle.

Leslie Doyle Mann says:

In December 2009, the Animal Rescue League of Boston received a call from animal control about a dog lying in a wooded area near Turtle Pond Parkway. When rescuers arrived at the scene, they found a seriously injured, emaciated female pit bull whom they named "Turtle" after the road where she was found. Turtle was taken to Tufts Veterinary Hospital, where veterinarians worked all night to stabilize her. Turtle had been used as a "bait dog" to train dogs for fighting, and suffered around sixty bite wounds and infection. Bait dogs are commonly discarded after a life of cruel and inhumane treatment; veteran rescuers called it one of the worst cases of animal cruelty they'd ever seen.

Turtle was actually one of the lucky ones, because unlike most bait dogs, she was found and rescued. After I read her story in the paper, I wanted to help. My goal was to raise money for Turtle's medical expenses, and to raise awareness that sadly, dog fighting is still going on right in our own backyards.

I wrote press releases and was interviewed by local newspapers and small TV stations. However, creating the video about Turtle and sharing it through Facebook and other channels was by far the most effective way to spread the word. We interviewed one of the veterinarians who treated Turtle, as well as Deb Vogel, one of the volunteers who saved Turtle that night and transported her by ambulance to get emergency care.

We posted the video to YouTube and other sites, and spread the word through Facebook animal activist groups and doggie playgroups. Within a week more than 2,500 people had viewed the video and we raised around $6,500 for Turtle's medical expenses.

When I started, initially I was focused on getting TV news coverage, which was very difficult to break into. However, I realized that we could use social media to get a compelling message out with a clear call to action in a more direct manner than we ever would have through a short snippet on the news.

In addition to the money we raised for Turtle's medical care, we also received many inquiries about adoption. We practically sold out seats for a spinning fundraiser that was held at Wellesley's "Spynergy" spinning studio and sold approximately 200 Turtle t-shirts.

I'm not a professional fundraiser or animal expert. I just read about Turtle in the newspaper and decided to do something to help her, so I didn't have a lot of experience answering questions. In the first interview I did, I found there was room for error in my responses. I studied the news clip afterward, and made changes the next time around to make my answers more succinct and clear. It was very hard not to get emotional when talking about Turtle's story. The first time this happened it made me nervous on camera. But I realized that it's okay to be human and to not cover up those emotions.

Three months after being rescued by ARL, Turtle was thriving in her foster home. Deb Vogel, one of Turtle's rescuers, says, "she looks like a different dog - she just looks amazing."

Animal Rescue League of Boston - www.arlboston.org

Try Podcasting

Podcasting is another way to get the word out about your organization. Even though the term might sound "techie," podcasting is really just a way of publishing sound files to the Internet. The term is sort of a combination of Pod (in honor of Apple's iPod) and broadcasting. However, contrary to popular belief, you don't need an iPod to listen to a podcast. All you need is software or a device that can play audio files.

Podcasts are just MP3 files, so you can listen to them using any software that can play MP3s. Sometimes you'll see the term podcast used to describe broadcasting video data as well, although many other names are often used, such as video podcasting or videocasting.

You can be a guest on an existing podcast or start a podcast of your own. If you want to be a guest, you can do a Google search for terms like *animal podcast* or *pet podcast*. You can also visit sites like iTunes and Blog Talk Radio and search for shows related to animals.

I do a podcast called "Take Me Home" for Pet Life Radio (www.petliferadio.com/takeme.html). In each episode I showcase a pet available for adoption at a shelter or rescue. I interview a foster parent, employee, or shelter volunteer to share the animal's story. The podcast radio network has a widget to download the podcast, and the show has been downloaded more than 200,000 times. The show has actually had more downloads than any other show on the Pet Life Radio network, which I view as a small victory for homeless pets!

If you want to be a guest on "Take Me Home" and talk about one of your adoptable pets, I'd love to hear from you! Just contact me and tell me you read about the show in *Publicity to the Rescue.*

You also can do a podcast of your own. When you have a show, people can "subscribe" to your podcast through sites like iTunes. When you put your podcast online, the "podcatcher" tells your subscribers that the new broadcast is available. The main thing that makes podcasting different from just putting an audio recording on your Web site is that you can publish (podcast) a show. People sign up to receive your shows automatically without having to go to your site to download it.

As an addition to a Web site, a podcast is useful to your visitors only if you have something to say that's worthwhile. Many people try one podcast and view it as a big waste of time because they don't get many listeners. However, like an e-mail newsletter, you have to work to build up an audience. Most successful podcasts have a lot in common with an e-zine or an online magazine. Successful podcasts are produced regularly and have interesting stories or something unique, such as interesting guests or provocative opinions.

It actually doesn't take long to record and upload a sound file and it's a great way to increase the audience for what you do. Of course, like anything computer-related, there's a learning curve with learning to record audio. It's more challenging if you're trying to record over the phone, although there are some software programs you can use with Skype that make the process easier. If you're just recording yourself and not doing a phone interview, creating a basic audio recording on your computer is quite simple. You need:

1. A microphone that plugs into your computer
2. Software to record your voice

Many computers come with a microphone that plugs into the little microphone jack on your computer. Some newer microphones plug into a USB port. Personally, I prefer a headset/microphone combination, so I don't accidentally move away from the microphone while I'm speaking. For recording, I have used a free software program called Audacity, which is fairly easy to use. It is *open-source* software, which means it's free. Versions are available for Microsoft Windows, Mac, and Linux users and you can download it here:

http://audacity.sourceforge.net/

Podcasts and most downloadable audio are saved in MP3 format, so you'll need to download the separate LAME encoder add-in for Audacity, because exporting to MP3 is not built in. It's also free and available here:

http://lame.buanzo.com.ar/

Getting your microphone to work on your computer depends on your setup; you'll want to consult the instructions that came with your microphone. Once your hardware is set up and your software is installed, you can just open Audacity. You'll see a big red "record" button, and not surprisingly, you click on that to make a recording. Do a few test recordings and see how your voice sounds. Click the big green "playback" button to listen to your recording, and before you know it you'll have your first podcast!

Case Study: Angel Acres and Homeward Bound Rescue League

Here's a case study that shows how a PR firm used audio and video to encourage people to help a horse rescue win a contest and get more foster homes for a dog rescue.

Scott Lorenz, the President of Westwind Communications says:

We have used audio and video to help a horse rescue and a dog rescue. In the case of the horse rescue, our goal was to get national attention and direct people to vote in the Zootoo million-dollar shelter makeover contest. In the case of the dog rescue, we were urgently trying to get new foster homes because the shelter was overwhelmed with a hundred or so new arrivals from a puppy mill. It was either find homes for the dogs, or they would be put down.

In the case of the horse rescue, I used YouTube to help Angel Acres Horse Haven Rescue make it to the top ten in a one-million-dollar shelter makeover contest sponsored by a Web site for animal and pet lovers called Zootoo. As part of the effort, I commissioned an emotional song and combined that with photos of horses and compelling on-screen copy. Our goal was to create a movement to support the online voting effort for the horse rescue. It worked; people who saw the video were moved to vote for Angel Acres and pass along the video to their friends.

We included the video in our press releases by adding a link to YouTube on the release. We used Expert Click and PR-Inside to distribute the release. Both services allow a video to be included or embedded with the press release. Angel Acres made it to the top ten, received a lot of media attention, and was awarded several thousand dollars.

I was the publicist for a dog rescue called Homeward Bound Rescue League, which desperately needed to find foster homes after they received an influx of dogs from a puppy mill. I sent press releases to my Detroit area media contacts. Because almost everyone has a dog, they could relate and they really jumped on the bandwagon to help get the word out. It helps if you know the media. Over the years I've gotten to know which newscasters own which type of dog. (I don't know them all, but I know about a dozen of them!)

One issue we had was that the publicity was so successful that the small rescue couldn't handle the response. When the media puts out an APB, you need to be able to handle the calls and e-mails. Homeward Bound was overrun with calls. The poor lady who was handling it finally turned her phone off because it was too much. However, they did recruit foster homes and hundreds of dogs have been saved.

Angel Acres - www.angelacreshorsehavenrescue.com

Homeward Bound - www.hbrlmi.com

Westwind Communications - www.westwindcos.com

Use the Celebrity Factor

Almost anything a celebrity does makes the news. You can take advantage of that and ride on their publicity coattails. Think about the George Foreman grill, for example. There was nothing unique or even particularly interesting about this kitchen appliance until they tacked George's name on it. Now it's been selling for years, even though you could argue that George's star has faded somewhat.

You can get a major boost in your publicity efforts if you include a local or national celebrity in your activities. If a celebrity adopts a pet from you, see if you can get a photo. Even if you attend a conference or seminar, if there's a celebrity there, ask if there's a way to get a picture and permission to send it to your local newspaper. It seems odd, but even standing next to a celebrity can give you instant credibility.

Many celebrities will give you an autograph if you write to them, and then you can turn around and raffle the autographed item in a fundraiser. If you're having an event, see if you can get a celebrity to participate. You'd be surprised who knows whom. One of your volunteers may be related to or know someone famous who loves animals. You never know if you don't ask.

You can find information about contacting celebrities in a number of ways:

- A simple Google search. Some celebrities have Web pages with information on how to get in touch with their publicist or assistant.

- Twitter. Amazingly enough, some celebrities actually do respond on Twitter.

- The Internet Movie Database (www.imdb.com) has a tremendous amount of information on stars in movies and TV shows. If you subscribe, you may be able to get contact information as well.

- Discussion boards. Many autograph collectors chat and share information about how to contact celebrities.

- Books or Web sites that list contact information. Some libraries have books with contact information.

A couple of Web sites also have databases you can pay to search.

- www.contactvip.com - $2.95 for a 7-day trial, then $9.95/month

- contactanycelebrity.com/cac/ - $1 for a 7-day trial, then $29.97/month

Publicity in Action

Case Study: Ken-Mar Rescue

Here's a case study that explains how Ken-Mar Rescue in California used the celebrity connection to promote an event.

Founder Martie Petrie says:

We held a local fundraising event called Brunching with the Stars, with a welcome speech delivered by Linda Hamilton. At $500 per ticket, we were targeting a specific donor base for a specific reason; we wanted to identify who our potential long -term donors were to ensure they could be rewarded for their contribution to our cause. It is said that 80% of a nonprofit's donations come from 20% of its donors; 10% of them are individuals (the other five-percent and five-percent are grants and foundations). We are trying to grow our core, long-term donor base.

Starting four to five months in advance, we wrote press releases (every two weeks to weekly, to days before the event), posted to Twitter and Facebook (almost daily), sent three to five newsletters, and did a local television spot.

We tried to do PSA spots with local radio stations, but didn't have much luck. We did manage to get into the "Pet Press," which is the local bible on all things pet. They ran a story as part of their upcoming events page.

We made flyers and distributed them to the caterer to give away at the host table in both of their restaurants (Beverly Hills and Silver Lake) and to the wine purveyor for her wine boutique store. These flyers were a win-win. They were geared for our target audience, included all logos of the three to four main donating companies, and showed their clients that they "gave back" to the community by supporting nonprofits.

Probably our most successful approach was getting the main donating companies to promote through their e-mail databases, their Web sites, and to their direct clientele face-to-face. This promotion gave Ken-Mar Rescue access to their closely held databases, which we would not have been able to access any other way. We weren't afraid or shy to promote unabashedly anywhere and everywhere, whether we were at a mobile pet adoption or standing in line for food at the grocery store. We let everyone know what we were doing.

We were able to negotiate donations from the following: caterer (food and services), wine, venue, photography, and videography. All of these services were added to thousands of dollars in donations. On top of that we were able to raise more than $3,000 from the event itself and get free publicity in the local press, which will introduce Ken-Mar Rescue's work to potentially hundreds, if not thousands of potential adopters, fosterers, and volunteers.

In addition, the Linda Hamilton Fan Club heard about her support of our cause and did a Facebook fundraiser four months later. They chose one of our long-term residents, Buddy, as their mascot and raised $1,000 for Ken-Mar Rescue. The group continue to support us through votes in pet-related competitions for funding and supplies on Facebook.

One thing that's difficult in working with celebrity "star dust" is worrying about whether a celebrity (or group of celebrities) can commit. An event takes months of planning and celebrities and their publicists can be reticent to commit more than thirty days in advance because of the uncertainty of juggling many other responsibilities. That doesn't give you enough time to pull off an event. You certainly don't want to promise a celebrity's fan base that their favorite celebrity is planning to be at the event, sell tickets to them, and then not deliver. That would be a fiasco!

Additionally, tying your organization's image to a celebrity in this day and age can be a dual-edged sword. Sometimes a celebrity's loyalty to a cause can be short-lived if they move on to something else, which can leave your non-profit in the lurch.

Although having a "name" support you can get you more press coverage, we've also seen too many celebrities crash and burn, and they can take the credibility of your organization with them. Of course, that can happen with corporate sponsorship, but to a lesser extent. Nonprofits are less impacted by corporate scandals than they are by a the actions of the big name that sits on your board of directors or headlines your next fundraiser.

Ken-Mar Rescue: www.kenmarrescue.org

Work Your Blog

A blog can be added to your Web site or can even be your entire Web site all by itself. At the most basic level, a blog is simply a date-based Web site where people can add comments.

From a technical standpoint, one of the primary advantages of a blog is that it is easy for people with little or no technical background to add posts quickly. Postings on a blog are almost always arranged in chronological order, with the most recent additions featured most prominently.

Because creating a blog is so easy, blogs have proliferated throughout the Web. Literally hundreds of thousands of blogs are online, covering every imaginable topic. In fact there's a whole "blogging community" online that you can be a part of simply by connecting with other bloggers. Links are the "currency" of the Internet. The more links you have to your blog or Web site, the more likely people are to visit. Having a lot of incoming links makes it easier for humans and search engines to find you, so making friends with other bloggers can be helpful.

Your blog will not be alone out there in cyberspace. Literally hundreds of millions of blogs are vying for attention, with about 150,000 new blogs created every day. If you decide to start a blog, you need to make a commitment to it. For every interesting, literate blog, there are thousands of abandoned, boring, trivial, and pointless blogs. The thing that people seem to forget amidst the "cool new idea" of blogging is that a blog requires you to put something in it. If you are burned out on writing, or think you'll run out of things to say on your topic, don't bother starting a blog.

Guest Post or Tour Other Blogs

If you are the shy, retiring sort, the idea of going out and rustling up attention face-to-face at events like networking meetings may seem intimidating. But you can "virtually" visit other people's blogs and share your message in writing by guest posting or even doing a "blog tour," which is really just a series of guest posts on related blogs.

For people like me who like to write, guest posting is a great alternative to face-to-face networking. Like having an event, it helps you get the word out about your organization, but guest posting means you don't have to leave your house. Instead of attending the local chamber of commerce meeting or networking roundtable, you "visit" blogs and network there instead.

When you guest post, you get to meet people in another blogger's community and have the opportunity to tell them about what you do. Another often-overlooked advantage of blog tours is that inevitably the blogger will link to your Web site. Remember that in the eyes of Google and other search engines, incoming links are a good thing. So from a search engine standpoint, your blog tour keeps giving "link love" long after the official tour is over.

The way it works is that you contact blog owners and pitch an article idea. You also can volunteer to answer commenter questions for a day. If you want to do a tour, the only difference is that you line up a series of blogs to post, and then promote on your own blog that you are going to touring. Each day, you make a "stop" at a different blog.

The advantage to the blogger is two-fold:

1. The blogger doesn't have to write a post.
2. The blogger gets a new perspective and the benefit of your expertise. For example, if you know a lot about dog behavior and tour pet blogs, you may be able to add a new perspective on the topic.

You may already be aware of blogs that would be interested in your guest posts. If not, you can use blog search tools such as Technorati.com and Google's blog search (http://blogsearch. google.com). Ideally, you'll want to guest post on popular blogs with a lot of visitors. Popular blogs with faithful readers tend to have a lot of comments. You also can get some idea of traffic rankings by going to www.Alexa.com and typing in the URL.

Blog tours do have disadvantages. One is that you aren't connecting in person with your supporters (although you can connect virtually, particularly if you offer to answer questions or comments). Another is that you won't get media coverage as you might with a live event that has been properly planned.

You may not see immediate results in the form of donations or inquires, but done consistently over time, all those incoming links from your guest posts will increase your visibility online. And the more visibility you have online, the more likely you are to attract supporters, donations, and adopters!

Publicity in Action

Case Study: Austin Humane Society

Here is a case study about how an advertising agency used an integrated strategy to help the Austin Humane Society stand out.

Suzanne Kyba, Vice President, Brand Strategy at Door Number 3 says:

Our goals were to help the Austin Humane Society brand stand out among the dozens of Austin-area shelters, increase donations in the midst of a recession, increase animal adoptions, and educate the community about the shelter's various educational, support, and health initiatives.

Instead of relying on the typical approach of fear and guilt to motivate adoptions and donations, we focused on the animal's personalities and the lifelong bond and emotional connection between pet and owner, as well as the impact animals and people have on each other. The new brand positioning stems from the idea of transforming lives, both human and pet. From there, we created the tagline and rallying cry: "Unleash Hope."

Once we had the positioning in place, we developed custom online tools to showcase the pets, highlighting aspects of their character, personality traits, habits, and special tricks. We also recruited over 100 Austin-based bands to donate songs, which we matched with animals to better reveal their personalities. And in order to provide an entertaining and educational glimpse into the population-reducing benefits of feral cat trapping, we also created an online game called Trapcat! which is very popular.

Another key component of the campaign was a series of four humorous videos we produced featuring animals speaking with each other about the various needs, perceptions, and misconceptions about shelter animals. These videos continue to be distributed internationally via video-sharing sites and pet blogs, and will also air on television.

The award-winning initiative worked best as an integrated campaign; each component had its own effect. The direct mail piece delivered more than a 100% increase year-over-year in donations, the videos generated some great buzz and were picked up by a Canadian animal organization and run on TV, TrapCat! and the custom animal adoption grids have won awards and recognition by other animal organizations throughout the country for their innovative approach, and the posters have helped to create strong awareness throughout Austin.

Of course, soliciting donations in the midst of a recession is always a challenge, but we achieved great results:

- A 30% increase in spring adoptions, year-over-year
- A 100% increase in holiday donations, year-over-year
- Online donations nearly doubled within a year of the campaign launch.
- The new AHS Web site is being cited as an industry model by the national pet adoption software, PetPoint.

Our mission was to define the AHS brand in an overcrowded marketplace with dozens of other animal organizations vying for the same attention. Fortunately for us, AHS has an amazingly unique organization, with dedicated, smart, passionate people, and they gave us a tremendous amount of freedom and flexibility to push the boundaries in our concepts and execution.

Austin Humane Society: www.austinhumanesociety.org

Door Number 3: www.dn3austin.com

Use E-mail and Autoresponders

The term autoresponder is bandied about a lot by people online. Many marketing and business "gurus" say you need an autoresponder, but often you don't see a good explanation of exactly what an autoresponder is or how it can be used.

At its simplest, an autoresponder is an e-mail that is sent out automatically. Some people set up an "out-of-the-office" message that replies to incoming e-mail when they are on vacation or otherwise unavailable. That outgoing e-mail is called an autoresponse.

Autoresponses are almost always used when you buy a product online. In that case, when the transaction is complete, the shopping cart sends you an e-mail with your receipt. Sometimes you may receive other follow-up messages after you ask for information or buy a product.

These follow-up e-mails are written beforehand, so the business owner doesn't have to take time to send an e-mail every time someone buys something or asks for information. Instead, the business owner uses autoresponder software to set up a sequence of e-mails that are sent at regular intervals.

Autoresponders can be used to generate leads, as well. For example, when a person signs up for my National Association of Pet Rescue Professionals newsletter, they give us an e-mail address. Every other week, they get a new issue of the newsletter. My autoresponder software manages the subscriber list, so I don't have to add and remove names myself. It also sends the newsletter out to everyone on the list.

Sending a newsletter is just one way to use an autoresponder. You also can use autoresponders to send out a sequence of e-mails, such as an "e-course," or special reports. In this case, you write a series of e-mails and the autoresponder software sends the e-mails at the intervals you specify. For example, people who visit my author training site can get a free seven-part e-course on book publishing.

When you have an autoresponder sign-up form on your Web site, you are essentially asking for permission to send information later. Maybe it's your newsletter or maybe it's a request for donations. No matter what you send, with an autoresponder you can educate and inform people about your services. As you send people good information over time, you establish trust. People are more likely to donate or adopt pets from people they know, so adding an e-mail autoresponder to your publicity arsenal can be an inexpensive way to get the word out.

Publicity in Action

Case Study: Humane Society of Memphis & Shelby County

Here's a case study that shows how the Humane Society of Memphis and Shelby County (HSMSC) used e-mail, word of mouth, and other internal communication to promote its dog-walking program.

Katie Pemberton, PR account manager and volunteer dog walker for the Humane Society of Memphis & Shelby County, says:

The overall goal of the dog-walking program was regular, consistent socialization, playtime, and exercise for HSMSC's resident dogs. The publicity factor was an unexpected benefit of the program. HSMSC dog walkers adopt pets, foster pets, and serve as HSMSC's cheerleaders among their friends, families, companies, and spheres of influence.

The program grew from 25 volunteers to more than 150 over approximately four years. E-mail and in-person word-of-mouth were the major communication tactics for growing the program. Communicating with volunteers is essential too and that is done via e-mail and HSMSC's Facebook fan page. Volunteers are kept apprised of adoptions, events, and other happenings using these two tools.

The word-of-mouth press we have received from our volunteers has been and continues to be vital to getting the word out, but we have recently ramped up PR efforts and are working on story pitching and news releases.

As most people involved with nonprofits know, a major challenge in retaining volunteers is helping them to feel attached and invested in the organization. We set up a system where a leader is in charge of the team of walkers every night. Now that the program is larger, dog walkers socialize dogs once daily and twice on Sundays.

Four years ago, only 25 dog walkers were taking the dogs out fairly sporadically. Since then, that number has increased to more than 150 walkers, all on a regimented time schedule. Having more dog walkers gives the dogs more exposure to socialization experiences and exercise, and improves their quality of life. A strong corps of dog walkers also enhances the organization's marketing, foster, and adoption efforts. Our volunteers have also helped set up programs like The Taz Fund, which funds surgeries above and beyond typical expenses, and Anakin's Buddies, a program that allows volunteers to "sponsor" a dog of their choice, paying for that animal's adoption fee. Additionally, volunteers frequently post animal photos and share their volunteer experiences on Facebook, which is great exposure for HSMSC that takes up none of our time or funds.

We constantly improve and update our dog-walking program, making changes such as the addition of wearing a mandatory t-shirt so that staff can easily identify volunteers, implementing training regimens for dogs with behavior issues, streamlining the process, etc.

I believe HSMSC's dog-walking program is the only one like it in the nation. I personally have never had such a well-organized volunteer experience in *any* nonprofit. It speaks to the importance of internal communication. When you're a nonprofit, much of your internal communication will be directed not only to your employees, but also to your volunteers, and our volunteers are a major element of our PR campaign.

Humane Society of Memphis and Shelby County -
    www.memphishumane.org

Obsidian PR: www.obsidianpr.com

Hold a Press Conference

You might think a press conference is just for presidents and world leaders, but there are situations when holding a press conference could make sense for your organization. If you're involved in a controversial situation, you may want to use a press conference to "clear the air" and clarify your position.

Don't hold a press conference if there's no real reason to do so. If nobody shows up, it's just embarrassing. But if you're being bombarded by calls about a newsworthy situation, setting up a press conference can save you a lot of time and actually net you more publicity. A press conference can heighten interest in a news story and actually increase the number of media outlets that cover it because news organizations are notoriously competitive.

If you opt to do a press conference, first you need to decide on a location and a date. Ideally, the place you select should be easily accessible and have audio and video technology, like a meeting room. The media is least likely to show up for an event on a Monday, Friday or the weekend, so try to avoid those days. Also, mornings tend to be better than afternoons because of deadlines.

Next, you need to invite the press to the event. You can do a press release or "media advisory" that lets members of the press know what you plan to talk about and who will be presenting. As with a press release, you should include the five Ws and the H.

You also can add information about the event to your Web site and include an outline of the information that will be covered. Or you can create a special press kit that you give to all attendees beforehand or at the press conference itself.

Make sure you are really clear on the story you want to tell and that your spokesperson is prepared. You may even want to do a "dry run" or rehearsal before the big day to make sure everything is ready. At the event, allow time for Q&A so the media can get all of their questions answered.

Publicity in Action

Case Study: FiXiT Foundation

Here's a case study that shows how the FiXiT Foundation used multiple media to get the word out about the benefits of spaying and neutering.

Dr. Kellie Heckman says:

FiXiT Foundation is a 501(c)(3) tax-exempt nonprofit founded in Norfolk, Virginia. FiXiT's mission is to revolutionize spay and neuter services by identifying and implementing tactics that will motivate the previously unreachable pet owner population. To start, we are testing our innovative strategy on St. Croix, in the U.S. Virgin Islands, a closed population of companion animals with a significant overpopulation problem.

We surveyed people and learned expense and lack of motivation were their primary reasons for not spaying or neutering, so we developed materials that emphasized the low cost of the surgery and promoted a spectrum of motivational messages.

We are using a variety of media to infiltrate the community, including multiple Internet-based sites; 60% of those sampled are on Facebook and Internet was chosen as the most commonly used media. We have used newspaper, radio, Facebook, Google, posters, yard signs, and magnetic signs on public transportation vehicles, in addition to sending regular press releases to both local St. Croix and national press.

This media blitz is promoting a spay/neuter clinic that FiXiT Foundation launched in February 2011 in collaboration with a private veterinary practice and the local animal shelter, which offers low-cost spay/neuter for $25. We are starting by charging the public, but will change the offer over time to include incentives and ultimately offer the procedure for free.

We will continue the "The Final Fix" over the next several years, determining which strategies are the most effective at increasing demand for spay/neuter. Ultimately, we hope to share the lessons we have learned and the challenges we have had to overcome with spay/neuter programs in the continental U.S. and on other islands. This will allow FiXiT Foundation to take spay and neuter to the next level.

FiXiT Foundation: www.fixit-foundation.org

Form Alliances

A tried and true way to get more publicity "bang for your buck" is to partner with a for-profit business or other organization. With both of you working together, you double the opportunities for media exposure.

Many fundraising events involve partnership or sponsorship by a for-profit business. For example, you might seek sponsorship to help offset costs for one of your events. When you partner with a business you both benefit from increased publicity opportunities.

The goal of sponsorship is for it to be a win-win between you and the business. As the charity/nonprofit, you get help with the expenses of the event and the business gets publicity and advertising exposure. The more benefits you can offer, the more likely it is to that you'll get sponsors.

Many rescues feel "shy" about approaching a company to partner with, but it's less intimidating when you understand what's in it for the business. From their standpoint, if they align themselves with your nonprofit, it makes them look like "good guys" in the eyes of their customers.

There's even a business term for this type of partnership: "cause marketing." In the business world, cause marketing is a big deal, because many studies have shown that people are more likely to buy products from companies that associate themselves with good causes.

If you get really good at publicity, you may find that companies will start approaching *you*. For example, a company may want a charity tie-in for an event. What's better than supporting a local animal shelter or rescue? Again, you have the advantage of all those cute fuzzy critters that look good on TV and in photographs.

Publicity in Action

Case Study: Philadelphia Animal Welfare Society

Here is a case study that shows how a group called the Monster Milers partnered with the Philadelphia Animal Welfare Society to encourage more volunteers to help exercise shelter dogs.

Monster Miler Carrie Maria says:

The Monster Milers are a group of runners who jog with dogs from the Philadelphia Animal Welfare Society (PAWS). The initial goal was to drive more volunteers into our running program. When we started, we just needed runners to take dogs out for jogs. We had no idea that it would morph into a program that's being copied all over the country!

Our main goals were:

1. Offer dogs in Philadelphia shelters a form of regular, vigorous exercise.

2. Bring about a sense of calm in the dogs, to facilitate quicker adoptions.

3. Attend annual running events and races to find loving homes for shelter dogs.

4. Encourage runners to adopt dogs for safety, friendship, and motivation.

5. Recruit more volunteers for Philadelphia's shelters, not only for running purposes.

6. Increase public awareness about the plight of the 30,000+ homeless pets that enter Philadelphia's animal shelters each year.

We formed unconventional alliances within the running community. We've networked with race directors, athletic clubs, sports shops, etc. We found that most of the time, rescues are "preaching to the choir." It's great to have a supportive base of passionate rescue advocates, but what happens when everyone you're targeting is already involved? By networking with the local running community and businesses, we tapped into a huge volunteer base. Only a handful of our volunteers had previously volunteered at an animal shelter. Most of them are shelter newbies, and that's the most exciting part for us, because we're expanding the community. Obviously, rescue advocates are a wonderful place to start, but if you can network into non-rescue circles, your impact is that much greater.

Simply being present and unconventional was incredibly effective. We set up tables along popular running trails, attend races with adoptable dogs, and wear "Adopt This Dog" shirts while we're out running with the dogs. People say we're everywhere. In fact, sometimes people call or e-mail saying, "I keep seeing runners with dogs in Old City with ADOPT ME vests on. Are you guys behind that? How do I get involved?"

The natural and effective model is to target pet-friendly audiences, but as I said, that can often lead to a tapped-out base. We created a new base. Our target base: runners who also want to do something good. Our slogan: "Make your runs count for more than just miles." We're connecting with people who want to do good and find something that is mutually beneficial.

Oddly enough, our biggest challenge was finding the time to manage all of the interested volunteers. We now have more than 200 people who still need to get through our small, hands-on orientations. The support from the local running community has been amazing. In fact, after a few big articles in *USA Today* and *Runner's World*, we were swamped with calls from all over the world, from dog-loving runners who want to set up something similar in their town.

The two biggest impacts from the publicity have been increased volunteers for Philly's shelters and quicker adoptions.

A lot of our volunteers may be new, but they're on *fire* for rescue now. It's amazing to watch. We figured we'd end up with a bunch of shelter volunteers who also happen to enjoy running. What we ended up with were a bunch of runners who became active in the shelter system. It continues to amaze me.

As far as adoptions, although it's hard to quantify why the dogs move out of the shelter and into homes, the shelter managers will attest to how the program is helping. From our *USAToday* article, PAWS manager Allison Lamond is quoted: "After a run, they're calm," says Lamond. "Their real personalities can shine through, and that has hastened the adoption of more than fifty dogs."

Philadelphia Animal Welfare Society: www.phillypaws.org

Monster Milers: www.themonstermilers.com

Go Offline

Many people get so excited about the idea of doing something new like creating a Facebook page that they forget about the publicity tools they already have. Offline publicity like flyers and newsletters still work. Many of your most ardent supporters may love getting things in the mail. And word-of-mouth is probably the most effective publicity you can ever get.

So think about what you already have that you can use to spread the word about your organization. Can you spread the joy and love with...

A **Web site or newsletter?** - Include information about fostering in your member newsletter and on your Web site. If you aren't already, let your supporters know how important foster families are to your organization. Include a plea for fosters on any communication you regularly create that people are likely to see. What about adoption paperwork? Member donation envelopes? Donation jars?

Flyers? - The ASPCA Professional site has a sample PDF from the Austin Humane Society that's really cute. It says "Be a Foster; Save a Life" and includes a foster volunteer FAQ. How many bulletin boards do you have in your community? Sure it might seem "old-school," but this type of simple offline education and promotion still works.

Volunteers? - Encourage current foster parents to spread the word about what they are doing. A lot of people are on social media and almost everyone has e-mail. It's amazing how a cute photo can spread around Facebook. Give your foster families material they can share with their friends. If you give someone a "sample tweet" in an e-mail, you just made it a lot easier for them to share the joy of fostering! Talk to your volunteers. You may have:

- Writers. Can they write materials?
- Designers. Could they take pictures of your adoptables?
- Speakers. Are they willing to do local presentations?

Sometimes incredibly talented people are close by and willing to help. It never hurts to ask.

Publicity in Action

Case Study: Riverfront Cats

Here's a case study that shows how a member of the Cat Network of South Florida used flyers to help promote spaying and neutering homeless cats in South Florida.

Cat Network member and community volunteer Christine Michaels says:

Initially, I wanted to raise awareness in my neighborhood about the plight of homeless cats and then branch out to surrounding neighborhoods so more stray cats would be spayed and neutered. At the same time, I am the founder of the Cat Network's Black Cat gala (Le Chat Noir), and our goal is to increase adoptions of homeless cats (especially black cats) in the entire South Florida region.

For the neighborhood effort, I began with a flyer but added a blog with facts and regular updates to add weight and credibility to the cause. I created a Web site called Riverfront Cats, which keeps visitors updated on the cats living within the Riverfront community.

The flyer was instrumental in getting residents to react and donate money or cat food. With the help of another Cat Network volunteer who moved into the building, we split up the responsibilities. She did the trap-neuter-release for most of the Riverfront cats while I took in ten kittens and went through the long process of cleaning, spaying/neutering, socializing, and getting them adopted.

At the same time, I learned that the developer wanted to "get rid of the cats" by trapping them and dropping them off at a state park. I immediately sent an e-mail alerting the association that "relocating" cats to a park is a euphemism for "dumping and abandoning," which is illegal under Florida law.

The old-fashioned grassroots flyer (with photos of the cats) was the most effective tactic we used. The flyer spoke directly to the residents of the neighborhood. I was able to recruit volunteers to help feed the cats and collect donations to get all of the cats spayed and neutered. In addition I always carry my Blackberry, business cards and flyers so if people see me feeding the cats and make inquiries, I'm ready. With the Blackberry, I can type contact information directly into my address book.

For the Black Cat gala, we leveraged all media: press releases, Facebook, e-blasts, banner ads, PSA announcements on TV and radio, and YouTube videos. Word of mouth and e-mails passed along to contacts was key to spreading the word. We achieved our goal of 300 attendees and raised $10K for the inaugural event. People are still talking about it and looking forward to the next one!

The Cat Network: www.thecatnetwork.org

Riverfront Cats: www.riverfrontcats.com

Keep Building the Buzz

Now that you have a lot of options for generating publicity, here's one final secret I'd like to share with you. Publicity success builds on itself. As you can probably tell from the case studies in this book, once you get publicity, the effect tends to snowball over time, if you work to keep spreading the joy.

So if you get great press, appear on TV, get on the radio, or anything else happens based on your publicity efforts, be sure to tell people.

In fact, you can even do a press release to say you got press! Sure it may sound silly, but it works. I once wrote a local press release saying that one of my Web sites was listed in *USA Today* as a "Top Site." Maybe it was a slow news day, but a regional paper ran my story!

Always share your publicity successes with your volunteers and post about it on social media too. Encourage retweeting and reposting. Your supporters love sharing good news. When they do that, they help build the buzz for you. And that helps the animals, which is, after all, what it's all about.

Good luck!

Index

About the Author
Susan Daffron

Susan Daffron is the founder of the National Association of Pet Rescue Professionals (www.naprp.com), which provides tools and information to help humane organizations save more companion animal lives. She also is the president of Logical Expressions, Inc., a book and software publishing company in Sandpoint, Idaho. She has authored 11 books including *Funds to the Rescue: 101 Fundraising Ideas for Humane and Animal Rescue Groups, Happy Hound: Develop a Great Relationship with Your Adopted Dog or Puppy* and *Happy Tabby: Develop a Great Relationship with Your Adopted Cat or Kitten.*

Two months after she and her husband moved to Idaho, Susan started volunteering at the local animal shelter. Her first week there, she adopted a sickly black puppy named Leia and nursed her back to health. She adopted two more dogs from the shelter and later adopted another dog from a rescue group in California and a cat from another local shelter.

Susan volunteered and subsequently worked as an employee and board member at the animal shelter for four years. Over the time she was involved, she used her graphic design and writing background to dramatically increase the visibility of the shelter in the community. She created hundreds of promotional materials, including banners, brochures, Web sites, forms, flyers, press releases, a new quarterly membership newsletter, and helped organize many fundraising events.

Susan also worked as a part-time veterinary technician at a low-cost spay/neuter clinic. There she learned more about veterinary issues, researched grants, and helped with software and administration issues.

A recognized expert on Web, editorial, design, and publishing topics, Susan has been involved in publishing since the late 80s.

About the
National Association of
Pet Rescue Professionals

The National Association of Pet Rescue Professionals is a membership association made up of people who are working for animal shelters, humane societies or rescue groups.

You can choose from free or paid membership:

1. FREE "Helping Paw" members receive a free report, weekly newsletter, and live access to monthly expert teleseminars.

2. Along with the newsletter and teleseminars, with your paid "Golden Paw Insider" membership you gain access to the private membership area of the NAPRP Web site, which has information and tools you need to save more pet's lives! Golden Paw Insider members receive tangible benefits in three important areas:

   - **Adopter Education**: two printed books for adopted pet owners, 100+ customizable articles, and more.

   - **Fundraising and Promotion**: fundraising ideas specific to humane and rescue groups, information on grants and grant writing, fundraising worksheets, templates for marketing materials, graphics, and more.

- **Administration and Management**: customizable business forms for tasks like faxes, telephone messages, volunteer management, and more.

The easiest way to learn more about the National Association of Pet Rescue Professionals is to visit us online at

www.naprp.com

Check Out More Books for Rescues!

Our books are available from LogicalExpressions.com or online booksellers, such as Amazon.com and BarnesandNoble.com. Books can be great fundraisers or educational tools. All our titles are available from Logical Expressions, Inc. at a 50% wholesale discount for qualified 501(c)3 non-profit buyers.

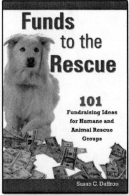

Funds to the Rescue:101 Fundraising Ideas for Humane and Animal Rescue Groups
by Susan C. Daffron
ISBN: 978-0-9749245-9-5;
LCCN: 2009905962
Multiple book award winner!
www.FundstotheRescue.com

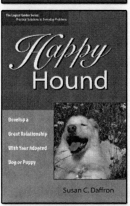

Happy Hound: Develop a Great Relationship with Your Adopted Dog or Puppy
by Susan C. Daffron
ISBN: 978-0-9749245-2-6;
LCCN-2006909898
www.HappyHoundBook.com

Happy Tabby: Develop a Great Relationship with Your Adopted Cat or Kitten
by Susan C. Daffron
ISBN: 978-0-9749245-3-3;
LCCN-2007906436
www.HappyTabbyBook.com

Check out our entire catalog of books at
www.LogicalExpressions.com/lebooks.htm

CPSIA information can be obtained at www.ICGtesting.com
Printed in the USA
LVOW051938230113

316973LV00003B/544/P